PRAYER, ASPIRATION AND CONTEMPLATION

from the Writings of John of St. Samson, O. Carm.,
Mystic and Charismatic

From the writings of John of St. Samson, O.Carm., mystic and charismatic

Prayer, Aspiration and Contemplation

Translated and edited by Venard Poslusney, O.Carm.

DISTRIBUTED BY
LIVING FLAME PRESS
BOX 74   LOCUST VALLEY, N.Y. 11560

ALBA · HOUSE   NEW · YORK

SOCIETY OF ST. PAUL, 2187 VICTORY BLVD., STATEN ISLAND, NEW YORK 10314

Library of Congress Cataloging in Publication Data

Jean de Saint-Samson, Brother, 1571-1636.
    Prayer, aspiration, and contemplation.
    Bibliography: p. 211
1. Spiritual life; Catholic authors; Collected works.
2. Prayer; Collected works. 3. Contemplation; Collected works. 4. Jean de St-Samson, Brother, 1571-1636.
I. Poslusney, Venard M., ed.   II. Title.
BX2349.J4513   248'.48'2   74-30340
ISBN 0-8189-0300-7

Imprimi Potest:
    Paul T. Hoban, O. Carm.

Nihil Obstat:
    Msgr. John H. Koenig
    Censor Librorum

Imprimatur:
    + Peter L. Gerety
    Archbishop of Newark
    January 17, 1975

*Designed, printed and bound in the United States of
America by the Fathers and Brothers of the Society of St. Paul,
2187 Victory Boulevard, Staten Island, New York, 10314,
as part of their communications apostolate.*

1 2 3 4 5 6 7 8 9 (Current Printing: first digit).

EDITOR'S PREFACE

The Writings of John of St. Samson are a valuable addition to the rich heritage of mystical literature accumulated over the centuries within the Church. Spiritual masters have recognized in him a beautiful exponent of the Art of the Prayer of Aspiration, even contributing to its further development as a spiritual means leading to contemplative prayer. His first-hand accounts and experiential descriptions of various forms of contemplative prayer are an exciting inspiration to all who earnestly seek a deep union with God in contemplation. Indeed, some of his accounts were delivered while obviously in deep prayer and ecstasy, thus reminding us of the impassioned prayers of Teresa of Avila in her *Interior Castle,* and the soaring flights of love so magnificently described by John of the Cross in his *Living Flame of Love.* Reading these Writings we become aware of the fact that we are listening to a true master of the spiritual life, offering many inspiring insights into the ways of growing in holiness. The language is not that of a theologian, but of a soul that has indeed experienced all that is there described. It is even bold and daring, but orthodox as the author describes all that is meant by a mystical marriage with Jesus Christ, the Bridegroom of the soul.

John of St. Samson is a commanding figure in the field of the mystical life and writes with great forcefulness. One of the most beautiful works in mystical literature is his *Epithalamium of Love* or *Bridal Song of Love,* quite orthodox, yet daring and remarkable in its originality. There he reveals his own interior life in the far reaches of the mystical marriage in terms of such intimacy that the reader is astonished at the boldness of the description. Yet he never errs or strays from the truth. Here we see all the folly of love for the divine Spouse, and the ineffable life of a soul that shares in the life of the Blessed Trinity.

What amazes us in all of this is the fact that the author was blind from the cradle and had no formal education, and yet we find unmistakable evidence of a free use of the gift of Wisdom in a high degree. But his greatest gift and charism was that of spiritual direction and this was recognized by the leaders of the Reform of Carmel in France, who made him the very heart of that spiritual renewal. That he was a great spiritual director is proven from the lives of those who became his disciples, whose sanctity and writings contributed so much to the golden age of spirituality of seventeenth century France.

His language is that of the Flemish and Rhenish Mystics and therefore requires some explanation. For this purpose we have included a Glossary to help the reader in his understanding of those terms that are characteristic of these mystical schools.

Venard M. Poslusney, O. Carm.

CONTENTS

PART I

LIFE OF JOHN OF ST. SAMSON
by Venard Poslusney, O. Carm.

CHAPTER I

LIFE OF JOHN OF ST. SAMSON

John of St. Samson was a humble blind Carmelite Lay Brother, who became one of the greatest mystics of the Church.[1] He lived during the golden age of spirituality in France when saints like Francis de Sales, Vincent de Paul, Cardinal Berulle, Jane Frances de Chantal, Louise de Maurillac, Madame Acarie (or, Ven. Marie of the Incarnation) were brilliant lights in the spiritual firmament. Though outwardly not gifted with the brilliance of his contemporaries, Brother John was highly endowed and talented. He possessed a keen intelligence and a phenomenal memory. These, together with an exalted holiness, enabled him to become a rare master in the direction of souls. Even though he was blind from the age of three, he managed to become a marvelous musician, especially as an organist. He was, moreover, a prolific writer on all phases of the spiritual life, especially the mystical life. Today he is considered the "Ruysbroeck of France",[2] and the John of the Cross of the Reform of Carmel in France.[3] To these titles we may add that of charismatic, for he manifestly possessed the gifts of wisdom, discernment, prophecy and healing.

John du Moulin, his name as a layman, was born in the historic city of Sens, France, December, 1571. The exact day is unknown. At the age of three, while convalescing from an attack of smallpox, thick crusts formed over his eyes and threatened to destroy his sight. On the suggestion of a stranger who claimed medical knowledge, his mother placed a patch of burning salve over the child's eyes. This brought on the complete loss of sight in the left eye and eventually in the right eye as well.[4]

John's early childhood up to the age of ten was a happy one in spite of his blindness. His father, Peter du Moulin, was a tax inspector in the city of Sens.[5] His mother, Marie d'Aiz, a very devout woman, was a descendant of the best families of that city. The family, therefore, lived in comfortable circumstances and held a position of honor in Sens. During these years John and his two brothers were carefully trained in the ways of piety and holiness by their devout mother. This came to an abrupt end when both parents died. John was ten years old at this time. Now an orphan, little John was sent to live with his maternal uncle, Zachery d'Aiz, in whose home he found children of his own age. Here he began to show a rare talent for music which was encouraged. In time he learned to play the organ and the spinet with great facility. At the age of twelve he was regular organist at the Dominican church for several years.[6] Besides these instruments he also played the flageolet, lute, flute, zither, oboe, viol, harp, 'mandore' (an old lute) and flute d'Allemand. It was no wonder that he was first to be invited to concerts in Sens or its environs. His teachers at this time were his uncle Zachary and the parish priest of St. Pierre-le-Rond, M. Garnier, who taught him the fundamentals of grammar. Besides learning the French poets, John also learned enough Latin to understand Latin authors and even the language when spoken to him. Unfortunately his formal education and literary training were not greatly developed. This did not prevent John from devouring every book he could have read to him. Among the spiritual works he preferred were the *Imitation of Christ*, the *Lives of the Saints*, the *Institutions* of John Tauler, and the *Mantelet of the Spouse* by the Flemish Franciscan, Franz Vervoort.[7] For a while Tauler's *Institutions* were his only reading. Here he found a hidden manna of which he could never have enough.[8] But the *Mantelet of the Spouse* had a profound influence on John's life. Above each chapter the author placed the words of St. Paul, "With Christ I am nailed to the cross." These words became John's motto for life.[9] A love for such strong spiritual food at about the age of fifteen is a clear indication of the strong character of John's soul and an authentic sign of holiness. A constant series of crosses may be found throughout his whole life, not the least of which was his blindness. In his last years his sincere wish to be totally nailed to the cross of Christ was truly fulfilled. On the last

day of his life, amid temptations from evil spirits, great physical
sufferings and an apparent abandonment by God, the words of St.
Paul were the last to be heard from his lips.

John's conversion to a life of perfection and high sanctity began
with the reading of the *Mantelet*. Blessed with a retentive memory,
he knew this work almost by heart and at once began to follow its
teachings. He gave up worldly amusements and associations, also the
reading of secular poets and historians. Much time was given to
mental prayer with generous use of the works of Louis of Granada.
His time was usually given to prayer, spiritual reading, visits to the
church and frequent reception of the sacraments of Reconciliation
and Holy Communion. His first biographers were convinced that
he had never lost his innocence in the matter of chastity.[10] At this
time, it seems that John was favored with some profound encounters
with God in love. The Lord was drawing him strongly to a life of
profound prayer, austerity, and poverty.[11] Realizing that he could
not follow the divine attraction for a deep and constant union with
God in the comfortable and worldly environment of his uncle
Zachary's home, the youth left home. In his blind condition and being
so young, John made the heroic decision to seek the hospitality of
various friends, going from one home to another. We know very
little about the ten years that followed and yet played such an important part in maturing his spirit. This much is known, John left his
relatives in order to pursue his new way of life without hindrance.
The only other fact known is that he continued his studies in music.

In 1597 John left Sens and went to live with his brother, John
Baptist and his family in Paris, near the church of St. Eustace. He
was now a young man of twenty-five, gentle, amiable, easy to get
along with and possessing a pleasing appearance. He spoke very
little of himself, and gladly spoke of God. Here he continued his
chosen way of life, spending long hours at the church in prayer,
attended the sermons — which lasted one hour in those days — and
was able to repeat them word for word on his return home.

After John's brother died, four years later, he moved to several
places for a brief stay, the last being a stay with the Prior of the
Canons Regular of St. Augustine near Notre-Dame. It was at this
time, in 1601, that John was accustomed to visit the monastery

Church of the Carmelites in the Place Maubert every day. Often the Prior of the Canons Regular was away for long hours on business and John had no key to the house. He therefore spent much time in the Carmelite Church where a young Carmelite student, Matthew Pinault, noticed him. Out of compassion he would gently lead John into the monastery for breakfast and thus a friendship grew up between the two. For several years he continued to spend his mornings in the Carmelite Church, arriving at six o'clock and often remaining there for six or seven hours on his knees, immovable and entirely lost in God. Sometime in the year 1604 John began to live at the monastery in return for giving lessons on the organ to a Father Peter Geoffray. Between Matthew Pinault, Peter Geoffray and John there grew a desire to share in the deeper aspects of the spiritual life, but it was John who was the master in the art of prayer and he began to teach them with great results. Elsewhere, a Father Philip Thibault was gathering about him a little circle of Carmelites interested in a renewal within Carmel. They were discouraged and were on the verge of leaving the Order when Father Philip met John briefly at the Place Maubert. Philip was deeply impressed by John's words and encouragement. According to Father Donatien, John's words "struck the heart of this Father (Philip) like a bolt of lightning and were so deeply engraved there that he not only joined the enterprise, but even became the leader of this reform."[12]

During the year 1606 John asked to be received into the Order and was accepted, though there were many misgivings about this on the part of the religious, yet the Provincial, Father Champcheurieux gave the permission. Without delay, John entered the novitiate at Dol, an ancient, historic city located on the northern sea coast of Brittany along the English Channel. He was at once given the habit and added to his baptismal name, 'St. Samson'.

Brother John of St. Samson easily blended his life with that of the community, though he refused to accept its relaxations, since it was not reformed. Each of the religious had his own temporal resources and disposed of them as he wished. As a layman his diet was more severe, and adapting to the community was one of many crosses the Lord provided. Because of the climate, and especially the marshes, many of the inhabitants were periodically attacked by a violent fever. Brother John soon fell victim to the fever and no remedies were effective against it. In this pitiable condition, consumed by fever yet refusing to give up his religious exercises, he was urged to say the prayer of St. Peter of Rome, who brought miraculous results to the fever-stricken in that city. "May the Lord Jesus, who cured Peter's mother-in-law of the fever which afflicted her, himself cure his servant of the fever from which he suffers. In the name of the Father, and of the Son, and of the Holy Spirit."[13] After going to Confession and Communion, John said the prayer with great faith, and was immediately healed. Ordered by the superior to say the prayer over others in the community, they too were cured. Later when the plague broke out in the town, one of the religious of the house was infected by it and through Brother John's prayers was cured.

His year of novitiate was soon over, and yet John had no Novice Master. When the Rule was read to him he understood it because, he later confessed, "God did not give me a Father Master to guide me, but fulfilled this office toward me himself in an excellent manner."[14] He was professed in 1607 at Dol. Already living in deep union with God and enjoying mystical prayer, John became a perfect model of Carmelite observance. At this time however, it seems that he was undergoing deep spiritual purification. Besides his bodily infirmities, he suffered from great dryness and darkness in prayer, and apparent abandonment by God. These seemed to be the final preparations for union with God in the highest state of the mystical life.

Around this time a new epidemic of the marsh-fever broke out and the people of the town came to the church asking for Brother John to pray over them. At the superior's order, Brother John was led into the church and said the prayer of St. Peter of Rome over each sufferer and ended by blessing them with the sign of the cross and sent them away cured.[15] When a servant of the bishop, Anthony de Revol, was cured, the bishop decided to investigate. After watching the ceremony of Brother John blessing the people, the bishop suddenly spoke up in a loud voice in the middle of the church, "Brother John, who made you so bold as to bless my people in my presence?" John replied, "Pardon me, your Lordship, I did not know you were present." Then the bishop accused him of abuse of power and fraud, and sharply rebuked him before the entire assembly, adding that his prayer was mere superstition. At this the blind Brother asked the bishop's leave to speak. "I beg your pardon your Lordship, but the prayer is perfect in its meaning. There is no superstition in it." Turning to his theologian, the bishop asked, "What do you think, Doctor?" The theologian replied, "The Apostles did not do any more than this. If we lived a life like that of Brother John, and if we had as much faith as he, we too would cure these sick people." After learning that Brother John only acted on orders of his superior, the bishop was finally convinced and won over by the holiness of the blind Carmelite. He concluded this scene with the words, "Very well, Brother John, I add to your obedience the command to continue curing the sick."[16]

There now sprang up a very close friendship between the bishop and the blind Brother. He often came to see him and to talk of the spiritual life. Gradually he fell under the spell of Brother John's inspiring instructions, and admired the sureness and authority with which he spoke about the divine truths, perfection and prayer. The bishop became the spiritual disciple of the humble, divinely inspired Brother.

During his first two years at Dol, John of St. Samson had many painful encounters with demons who often tempted and visibly tormented him, trying to choke and suffocate him. They appeared in the form of frightful beasts who scratched him and uttered chilling shrieks intended only for his ears. The marks of many scratches were plainly evident on his hands and face. His body too was covered with bruises as was testified by Father Matthew Pinault.[17] For the remainder of the thirty years of his religious life John of St. Samson was to have a running battle with demons. His enlightened faith, firm confidence, burning love of God, profound humility and unfailing patience were his shield. Sometimes during the most violent of these terrible trials, he would make fun of the devils and mock them. He would call them dogs and blind moles who were incapable of seeing God. At other times he treated them with contempt and scorn, and acted as though he did not feel their weakness at not being able to vanquish one who was armed only with confidence in God. Then he would send them back to hell to be punished by their accursed ruler, because they allowed themselves to be overcome by a mere nothing of a man.[18]

His regular duty at the monastery was to play the organ at Mass and Divine Office. On occasion he was also sent to help with the work in the kitchen. In time he developed a special apostolate among the sick and dying. On his visits he would carry with him a special cross inlaid with relics which he held before those in their last agony, helping them with truly inspired exhortations. All acknowledged that he did indeed possess a special gift for assisting the sick and preparing the dying for a happy and holy death.

In the city of Rennes, Father Philip Thibault had been elected Prior of the Carmelite monastery there in 1611 for the second time. He had already begun the Reform of Carmel and gathered around him Carmelites of proven virtue, among them, Brother John's friend, Matthew Pinault who was sub-prior and master of novices in the reformed community.[19] Now Father Philip invited Brother John to come and join the reformed Carmel of Rennes. Of course he had to make a new novitiate.[20] It was to be a year of severe testing.

Prudent by nature but also over fearful, Father Thibault had a certain distrust of the holiness which he recognized in the blind Brother from the very first time they met at the Place Maubert. He felt that the religious at Dol had paraded it too much. From now on, Brother John was to observe strict solitude. He was to remain in his cell and say his rosary like the other lay brothers, unless called by his few duties to play the organ in the chapel or to some other task in the monastery. No more visits to outsiders, no more spiritual conferences, not even charitable visits to the sick and dying.[21] The exact nature of the various trials to which he was subjected is not known, but their purpose was to test his humility and obedience. When speaking of these trials, Father Donatien says that they were not the least of the many trials to which he was subject in the course of his religious life.[22] After the year of novitiate he was tested for another year.

For John of St. Samson so much time for prayer was a heaven-sent gift. Hours were spent in contemplation. His mystic soul thirsted for this exalted union with the Beloved. Perhaps he had already reached the transforming union. The nature of his trials previous to this period, the perfection of his virtue and the state of mystical prayer which he described at Father Philip's request would seem to confirm this. Even as a lay person it was generally known that he received extraordinary graces which normally prepare the soul for the sublime state of the transforming union. He would often fall into ecstasy when some mystical work was being read to him.

However, the time came when God gave him a marvelous strength to sustain his divine action and to bear the violence of the fire of love with a steady evenness of soul. Henceforth, while his interior was plunged in the most delightful intoxication, a calm and humble exterior concealed from others all evidence of such mysteries. On occasions, however, the light that flooded his soul and the flames that consumed his interior were revealed externally by a certain radiance visible to all eyes. "In these extraordinary states," Father Donatien writes, "we often saw his face glowing and radiant with, I know not what kind of luminous ray, which used to be reflected from it. I myself witnessed it with a number of other trustworthy religious. No one can doubt the truth of this, since John himself, in his *Mystical Cabinet,* indicates that he often experienced this light which spread from the center of his soul to all his faculties, even to the exterior senses.."[23] Only God would know how far he progressed in this highest state of the mystical life during the remaining twenty-four years of his religious life.

Now Father Philip wanted definite proof of Brother John's method of prayer. He accused him of pretending to be a contemplative and dispensing himself from the common rules of meditation. He therefore ordered him to follow the example of the other young religious. John obediently set about meditating like any beginner, but the Lord would at once carry his mind and heart to an exalted mystical union with himself, thus making it impossible for him to use his mental faculties in meditation. Pretending unbelief when John explained this, Father Thibault ordered him to dictate an explanation of his method of prayer. Brother John composed a short treatise and described his prayer in the following words:

> My practice consists in a complete elevation of the soul above every created and sense object. During this time my soul is constantly occupied, steadfastly looking upon God

who draws me to a simple unity and nakedness of spirit. This
is called simple idleness. In this state I am passively occupied
in simple repose beyond everything that can be felt. I always
enjoy this in the same manner, whether I am alone and have
nothing to do, or whether I am occupied with something
interiorly in thought, or exteriorly in action.[24] This is what
I can say of my interior state. It is simple, naked, obscure
and without knowledge of God himself, in nakedness and
simplicity of soul, raised above all light that is inferior to
this state. In this state I cannot work with my interior faculties. They are all drawn together and fixed by the power
of the simple Divinity which binds them nakedly and simply
. . . in the highest part of the soul, above the soul in the naked
and obscure depths of the Incomprehensible. . . . There all the
faculties being gathered in unity of spirit, or rather in simplicity of spirit, attentively and steadily gaze upon God. . . .[25]

Unwilling to be the only judge in this matter, Father Philip
sent this treatise to Father Duval and Father Gibieuf of the Sorbonne in Paris, to the Jesuits at the college nearby, also to the
provincial chapter of the Capuchins. All approved it and admired it.
When he consulted the discalced Carmelites they too approved it
and added,, "Do not extinguish the spirit." Even with this approval,
Father Philip continued to test John's spirit with such frequent
and severe mortifications as would have broken the spirit of anyone
else less humble and virtuous. During all this time, John was
unfailingly obedient, humble, gentle and patient.

Now the reformer, Father Thibault, took the next step. He
wanted to set John of Samson before the reformed of Carmel as a
model and master of virtue. He did something that in most other
circumstances would have been rash and foolish. He made this
simple, blind lay Brother the actual spiritual master and director
of the monastery of Rennes. In so doing he made John of St.
Samson the guiding spirit of the whole Reform.[26] He was to continue in this capacity for the next twenty years, living most of
the time at Rennes. Matthew Pinault, the novice master, sent all
the novices to John every day for training and guidance in the
interior life and to absorb the true spirit of Carmel. In adapting
the methods of the spiritual life to the particular religious, John
was a prudent, but exacting master. Over the years these young

Carmelites eventually became Priors, Novice Masters, and some of them became Provincials and Definitors—all of them formed by the blind Master of Rennes, the soul of the Reform of Touraine. Many of them faithfully corresponded with him and sought continued guidance, such as Dominic of St. Albert, Leo of St. John, Bernard of St. Magdalen, Mark of the Nativity, Luke of St. Anthony and Angelus of St. Agnes.

Besides directing his Carmelite brethren, there were other religious, superiors and members of other communities who eagerly sought his guidance. Much against his will, his company and advice were sought by those of high station, like Queen Marie de Medici, mother of Louis XIII, by the Bishops of Rennes, Nantes, Dol and Saint Brieux, by the rector of the Jesuit College at Dol, Père Bertrix, by Monsieur de Cucé, president of the Parliament of Brittany and others. The Ursuline nuns and sisters of other religious communities also sought his spiritual direction. From all this we may conclude that God had indeed gifted Brother John with the special charism of being able to direct souls to a deep union with God.

Among the special privileges given him by the Lord was that of enjoying the physical presence of the Lord in the Eucharist for six or seven hours after Communion. This is the reason why the host is depicted on his breast in the picture frontispiece of this book.[27] Veiled reference to this may be found in his *Epithalame*, one of the most beautiful treatises in mystical literature. There he extends loving invitations to the Beloved to come to him under the Sacramental Species, to enter his garden full of spiritual perfumes. Another supernatural privilege he enjoyed was a certain supernatural instinct which made him aware of the presence of the Blessed Sacrament, or its absence. He also admitted to one of his superiors that God gave him the ability to discern the presence of priests and superiors even though they were among lay persons.[28]

Being an elect soul we expect him to be perfect in virtue. His outstanding virtue seems to have been charity. He had an extraordinary love for his brethren, especially for the sick and dying. There can be no doubt that he had a special gift for consoling and healing the sick. When confined to the Champ St. Jacques Sanatorium, he paid regular visits to the sick and dying. On numerous occasions both at Dol and at Rennes, he visited the sick and dying in their homes when his presence was requested. His words and his prayers were especially efficacious in assisting souls in their last agony. At the sound of his voice, their anxieties and terrors vanished and their souls were filled with hope and love, and even an impatient desire to see God. Austere toward himself, he was always deeply moved by the sufferings of his brethren and would employ every means to relieve their afflictions. Blind as he was, he did not hesitate to take upon himself all their burdens. His wise counsel showed broad understanding and an indulgent charity in the face of the difficulties and faults of his neighbor. This compassion for the needs of others was also shown to animals. He would never allow anyone to hurt them in his presence. In the winter, his room became a place of refuge for little birds during the night.

The long hours that John's mystic soul spent in prayer was common knowledge. Besides the hours of the day, he also devoted part of his nights to prayer, often spending only a few hours in sleep and that in his full habit. Even then, he slept so lightly that he hardly knew himself if he had slept. Often it was he who awakened the exhortator whose duty it was to call the religious for midnight Matins, but overslept because his alarm failed to ring. Despite his pre-eminence in the prayer of contemplation, as a Carmelite Brother, he devoutly said the office of lay Brothers common at that time, namely, a certain number of "Our Fathers" and "Hail Marys."

In our own time when we see a thrilling spiritual renewal being worked in the hearts of God's People by the Holy Spirit, it is interesting to note how the Gifts of the Holy Spirit were active in this great mystic. We have only to read the many profound mystical treatises he composed to see how his soul was filled with the gifts of wisdom, knowledge and understanding. There we see tangible evidence of the sublime contemplation he constantly enjoyed. The Holy Spirit enkindled the depths of his soul with a burning and consuming fire that extended its influence over all his faculties with an inexpressible impetuosity and pleasure. Sometimes with the permission of his superiors he would dictate his thoughts and inspirations for his own private reading and benefit, to give expression to the divine impulses and the flames of the mystical fire burning within him. This is especially evident in his *Contemplations* and *Soliloquies.* There addressing himself to God, he would say, "Of what use is it to be consumed in the fire of your love and not speak of it? Shall I be consumed in silence by a fire so sweet and delightful and not give vent to the flame of love in utterance"? He compared the intensity of this divine fire to those streams of fire that burst from certain subterranean volcanoes, and reduce all they encounter to cinders. When he was first subject to the influence of this all-consuming fire, it exerted unbelievable power in consuming all within him. But as he grew in simplicity and advanced further into the transforming union, this fire softened its rigor and produced in him a sweet kiss of love which he calls, "the Baptism of the Holy Spirit" in his *Book of Contemplations.*[29]

Once this divine fire is enkindled within a soul, he said, it never dies. It consumes all that belongs to the creature. At the same time it melts, changes and converts the soul into itself far better than fire melts and converts into itself the metals that are cast into it. Then the soul enjoys the glory of God in a certain measure even though it retains its created nature. Sometimes even the senses share in this glorious feast. In this state it seems to be in a constant ecstasy and rapture, not so as to be deprived of the use of its senses, but according to the highest part of the soul, in its substance, where it is completely lost in God.[30] Those who have passed through the passive purifications are then able to sustain the sublime effects of the loving Flame without being carried out of their senses.

In his association with others John invariably left a pleasant and delightful impression. What he said or did was usually accompanied by great wisdom and restraint. Even though his interior state and inclination might far surpass those around him, he was able to accommodate himself so well to the character of each person that he seemed to live a very ordinary life. In conversation John carefully observed prudence and simplicity. Simplicity was a definite characteristic of his union with God and thus made his conversation sincere and free of all simulation and false pretense. Equivocation, ridicule and duplicity he considered to be the plagues of courteous and Christian conversation. The foundation for all this was an unwearied and constant elevation of his mind to God together with detachment from all things. So he was able to leave everyone to his own ways and habits while at the same time firmly keeping his own, enduring the faults and mistakes of others without any interior hindrance or impatience.

With the approach of old age Brother John had to bear crushing bodily afflictions. Having had to rely most of his life upon his hearing, he now found that he was almost deaf. In the last eleven years he suffered greatly from ulcers on both legs. While the one leg healed, the sores on the other refused to heal. In the beginning of this illness he concealed it with great care, until he could no longer avoid limping thus drawing the attention of his superior. From this time on his dear friend, Father Joseph, was appointed to be his guardian. In the midst of a large community such as then lived at Rennes, the aged Brother now had to endure unfavorable criticism of varying kinds. While there were those who admired him, there were others who thought John's sanctity was a convenient kind of holiness. They said that he was being well fed, clothed in a fine habit and good shoes,[31] whereas he ought to be sharing the poverty of the house like the others. But John only accepted this consideration shown him by Father Joseph out of obedience and because he needed another habit, and also shoes and proper care in his illness. His critics made fun of his manner of speaking and the terminology he was accustomed to use. Some mimicked him. Others censured him when he was silent. If he spoke on spiritual subjects they accused him of wanting to be Father Master, or a preacher.[32] When he defended the truth against some error that his enlightened mind easily detected, they declared him stubborn. Sometimes he would inquire for news about a war, about the campaign against the Calvinists, or about affairs at the royal court. This curiosity provoked his opponents into a show of scandal at his supposed "weaknesses."

In the last week of his life he went to bed with a high fever, which eventually brought about an inflammation in his head and then spread to his chest. This eventually was the cause of his death. During the course of this illness he was constantly afflicted with great dryness of soul, a sense of abandonment, and a want of all feelings. He suffered acutely at not being able seemingly to make an act of love of God. He complained of attacks from the devils. Quite often his brethren heard him say, "With Christ I am nailed to the cross," an expression that was very dear to him. These were the last words they heard him pronounce. His last act was to raise the crucifix to his lips, and kiss it repeatedly. He died on Sunday, Sept. 14, 1636, the Feast of the Exaltation of the Holy Cross, the cross that he had cherished so much during his life. He was sixty-four years old.[33]

John of St. Samson left this world with a reputation for eminent sanctity, a heritage of admirable mystical writings and a group of fervent disciples who eventually spearheaded a reform in Carmel that spread throughout the entire Order. In the succeeding years, many cures through his intercession were recorded.[34] Within the monastery at Rennes John's confreres spoke of him as 'our blessed brother,' 'our saint.' Since that time a common tradition within the Order has considered John of St. Samson as 'venerable.' His cause for Canonization was never pursued, because many of the Carmelites thought a process was unnecessary. In their opinion the case was won before it was even begun.

All these eulogies, however, are private and do not have an official character. Although preparations were made for such a process, the cause was never officially entered into the records of the Sacred Congregation of Rites.[35]

1. **Dictionnaire de Spiritualité**, t. I; Art. **Ame**, by Père Leo Reypens, S.J., col. 464: John of St. Samson is "the most profound mystic of France." Also, Valerius Hoppenbrouwers, O.Carm., **Devotio Mariana in Ordine B.M.V. de monte Carmelo**... Rome, 1960, p. 215: "Outstanding among the greatest mystics of France."

2. **Revue d'ascetique et de mystique**, 1922, p. 252, note; article by Leo Reypens, S.J.

3. Sernin de St. André, O.C.D., **La Vie du V.F. Jean de St. Samson**..., Paris Poussielgue, 1881, p. 91. Henri Bremond, **Histoire litteraire du sentiment religieux en France**..., Paris, 1916-1936, Vol. II, p. 379; Pierre Pourrat, **La Spiritualité chretienne**, Paris, 1926-1928, Vol. III, p. 484; Titus Brandsma, O.Carm., **Carmelite Mysticism**, Chicago, 1936, p. 95.

4. Father Donatien of St. Nicholas, O.Carm., **La Vie, les maximes et partie des Oeuvres du Fr. Jean de St. Samson**, Paris Denis Thiery, 1651; p. 2. Father Donatien was a member of the same community and a close friend of John of St. Samson.

5. Father Joseph of Jesus, O.Carm., **Manuscript: Grand Carmes de Rennes. Vie de F. Jean de St. Samson, carme**; Rennes, 17th cent., pp. 195; cf. p. 9. Hereafter, this text will be referred to as **Ms. Joseph**. Most of the texts from this Manuscript may be found in Suzanne Bouchereaux, **La Reforme des Carmes en France et Jean de St. Samson**, Paris, J. Vrin, 1651; p. 490.

6. **Ms.** Joseph, p. 9, and Donatien, **op. cit.**, p. 3.

7. Bouchereaux, **op. cit.**, p. 127.

8. **Ms.** Joseph, p. 29, and Donatien, **op. cit.**, p. 4.

9. Sernin of St. Andre, O.C.D., **Vie du Ven. F. Jean de St. Samson**, Paris, Poussielgue, 1881; p. 11.

10. Sernin, **op. cit.**, p. 12.

11. Bouchereaux, **op. cit.**, p. 128.

12. Donatien, **Abregé de la Vie**, t. I, p. 3.

13. Donatien, **op. cit.**, p. 26; **Ms.** Joseph, p. 22.

14. **Ibidem, op. cit.**, chap. 7; this reference in Sernin, **op. cit.**, p. 45.

15. This entire account is drawn from the testimony of Matthew Pinault. cf. **Ms.** Joseph, p. 23. Father Donatien reproduces this account quite closely.

16. **Ms.** Joseph, p. 25.

17. **Ms.** Joseph, p. 25.

18. Donatien, **Abregé de la Vie**, p. 4.

19. P.W. Janssen, O.Carm., **Les Origines de la Reforme des Carmes en France au XVII Siecle**, Nijhoff, Hague, 1963; p. 53. Also, Bouchereaux, **op. cit.**, p. 144.

20. Janssen, **op. cit.**, p. 175.

21. Donatien, **Abregé de la Vie,** p. 5.

22. Ibidem.

23. **Op. cit.,** Chap. 13; also, **Abregé de la Vie,** p. 8.

24. This state is characteristic of souls in the transforming union. They are always aware of the divine Presence.

25. Donatien, **op. cit., p.** 50-51.

26. Bouchereaux, **op. cit.,** chap. 8, to be found in Sernin de St. André, **op. cit.,** p. 88-89. It was Father Joseph's conviction that "the life of the spirit, the life of a true Carmelite, poured into the veins of the new Reform through John of St. Samson as through a channel chosen by God." **Ms.,** p. 32.

27. **Ms. Joseph,** p. 30; Donatien, **op. cit.,** p. 81ff.

28. Donatien, **op. cit.,** p. 8.

29. Donatien, "**Abregé de la Vie,**" p. 8.

30. **Ibidem,** p. 8.

31. **Ms. Joseph,** p. 30.

32. **Ibidem,** p. 31.

33. **Ms.** Joseph, p. 69-72. Immediately after his death an artist was called in to make a mold of his face on plaster which was very successful. (Cf. Sernin of St. André, **op. cit.,** p. 329.) The portrait which appears in this book was made according to this death mask. Of all the portraits made of John of St. Samson, Father Joseph, his guardian, preferred this one, because as he said, it is "just like him." Cf. Sernin de St. André, **op. cit.,** p. xxii, footnote, n. 1.

34. Donatien, **Abregé de la Vie,** p. 13.

35. This was confirmed in a Letter sent to Father Venard Poslusney, O.Carm. by the Very Rev. James Melsen, O.Carm., Assistant General, on January 20, 1964: "The 'Causa' of John of St. Samson was never officially introduced to the Sacred Congregation, and as far as I know, there was never a real beginning of a Process."

CHAPTER II

HIS WRITINGS

Soon after John of St. Samson's appointment as spiritual director of the novices at Rennes, the superiors ordered him to compose exercises for their use. They realized that, with time, unless his instructions and spiritual counsels were written down, they would be forgotten. For this task, since he was blind, Brother John was given the services of the young religious to whom he dictated his thoughts. Many of the religious sought the honor of being one of his secretaries. They wished to profit by the hours of close association with him in order to obtain advice for their own spiritual life. Among the many secretaries that he had over the years, one of the most famous was Leo of St. John,[1] who later became Provincial, Preacher and Confessor to the King, who himself wrote many books on the spiritual life.

Father Joseph has left us an interesting account of Brother John's method of dictation. "It was a marvelous thing to see him dictating his works with such speed and without any previous reflection, that his copyists were quite fatigued by it. For it required great concentration in order to retain what he dictated and a quick hand to keep up with him. For his part, he dictated for whole days without growing tired. The hands of his copyists ached so much after having written down his dictation, that they could hardly move their fingers. It is a remarkable fact which I have noticed a number of times, that, when one of his secretaries could not remember what he had said in the beginning and asked him to repeat it, he was unable to recall what he had dictated nor was he able to repeat it again in such felicitous terms. I consider this an evident sign that the Divine Spirit was active in him, and that it was done without reflection. And he himself admitted to me several times that, after having written some treatises, he did not know what he had dictated until he heard it read back to him. If he could have had secretaries with him constantly, he would have dictated as many more treatises as he had already composed (*viz. he composed twenty-six books*)."[2]

From Father Donatien we learn that those works which he thus dictated, viz. "in an evidently ecstatic state," were intended for his own personal use, e.g., *The Soliloquies, Book of Contemplations* and several other mystical treatises. In them he reveals the depth of his interior life and the exalted mystical union he enjoyed with the Divine Spouse. There we see a soul raised to the greatest heights of the transforming union in unbelievable intimacy with God. One is reminded of the rare states of union that are described by Bl. van Ruysbroeck. John of St. Samson attempted to describe his experiences even though a mystic like St. John of the Cross, in a similar state, was content merely to give a brief description, because words fail to portray the reality. But Brother John wanted to describe these ineffable states as clearly as possible humanly speaking, so that he might re-live them in his writings. For he admitted, "I am afraid that God may abandon me, that I may become interiorly blind and so fall away from my present state. Even now I am anticipating such a misfortune with this remedy, if it should happen to me. In this way, my writings will be a kind of mirror for me. In them I shall see what I have been and the purity of dispositions from which I shall have fallen."[3]

When John of St. Samson began to dictate his writings, he was already in full command of his teaching and form of spirituality. These had two sources, *viz.* his wide reading and his personal experience. He was quite familiar with nearly all that one could read at that time. The Scriptures he knew thoroughly. He was very well informed on the teachings of the Fathers of the Church at least from published collections, such as the *Fleurs des Sentences,* or the *Psychagogia* of Louis Blosius.[4] Those whom he quotes most frequently are St. Augustine, St. Bernard, St. Gregory the Great and Denis the Areopagite. Quite often too there are quotations from St. Ambrose, St. Jerome, Cassian, Gregory Nazianzen. Less often we encounter St. John Chrysostom, St. Peter Chrysologus, St. John Climacus, Lawrence Justinian, St. Anthony, St. Hilarion, and St. Paul the Anchorite. All these writers and many others may be found in the collection of quotations from the Fathers which John assembled in an unpublished work entitled, *Plusieurs belles Sentences tant des Pères que de Seneque.* Here, surprisingly, we also find quotations from such profane writers as Seneca, Pythagoras, Cicero, Cassiodorus, and Boethius. This deference to pagan writers is nothing new, for it had its precedent in previous centuries which gave so many pagan writers honorable places in Christian culture.

It was not only the ancient writers of the Church whom he knew, but those of more recent centuries. He was very familiar with the writings of St. Catherine of Genoa "whose life and most wonderful *Dialogue* clearly explain all my writings."[5] He also read the writings of Jules Fatius, Father Pinelli, "Dame Millanaise" or Isabelle Christine Bellinzaga, whose *Breve Compendio* Cardinal Berulle adapted in French.[6] But it is quite surprising that he quotes neither St. Thomas nor St. Bonaventure.

Among Spanish writers we find Louis of Granada who was a guide for him in the practice of prayer, John of Jesus-Mary, and Arias whom he recommends to the novices for reading. Surprisingly he quotes very little of St. Teresa of Avila, whose works he had read, for he mentions them in his *Lumières et Regles de Discrétion pour les Supérieurs.*[7] Elsewhere, there are allusions to the *Way of Perfection* and the *Interior Castle.* The first French translation of Teresa's Works appeared in 1601 before John entered Carmel. But we have no information as to whether he "read" them at this time or not.

Brother John seems to have "read" little of St. Ignatius of Loyola, for there is no mention of him at all in his writings. For that matter, neither is there any mention of St John of the Cross. But we know that he had "read" St. John's *Works* from the following account of a meeting between Brother John and two Discalced Fathers written by Father Joseph: "The Provincial of the Discalced Carmelites, who had a Father Joseph with him as companion, came to lodge in this monastery. He had heard of the great sanctity of our holy Brother and so wished to speak with him. But Father

Joseph particularly spoke with him for a long time and asked him
if he had read the Writings of Father John of the Cross. John
replied that he had, and that they were very excellent, but added
that there was still another life beyond that (spoken of by St. John
of the Cross). Our Brother's treatise on the *Consummation of the
Subject in its Object* is proof of what he said. Father Joseph then
asked him for his rosary and persisted in asking until Brother John
was forced to give it to him. Even before their meeting he considered John of St. Samson a saint. Now after the conference he
had with him he was convinced of it."[8]

This interview took place about the year 1629, and the Works
of St. John of the Cross were known in France from the year 1621.
However, the spiritual formation of John of St. Samson, at least
from books, had already been accomplished long before that time,
perhaps even by 1606. In the years that he lived at Paris before
entering the Order, John came to know the works of the Flemish
and Rhenish mystics, also Denis the Areopagite, Louis of Granada
and Gerson. Hence he was well acquainted with Tauler's *Institutions,* Eckhart and Suso—on whose *Nine Stones* he composed a
commentary which is now lost—Ruysbroeck, Harphius and the
Flemish classic, the *Evangelical Pearl* translated into French by
Beaucousin. Other writers who influenced his spiritual development
were Denis the Carthusian, St. Gertrude, Louis Blosius whom John
resembles on a number of doctrinal aspects. Among contemporary
authors there were the works of Deschamps *Garden of Contemplatives,* John Moschus' *Spiritual Pasture,* Benet Canfield, the English
Capuchin and Constantine Barbanson. John had high esteem for
Barbanson and considered his doctrine very suitable to his spirit
and full of wisdom.[9] It was Barbanson who helped John to formu-
late his doctrine on the practice of aspiration. During this period
John also read the writings of Venerable Bede, and Hugh of St.
Victor.[10]

We have already seen how great an influence the *Mantelet of
the Spouse* by the Flemish Franciscan, Frans Vervoort had on
Brother John. It would seem that his interior life was to a great
extent cast in the mold of this beautiful and exacting work. There
he learned about the renunciation of created things, detachment

from self, from one's own will and judgment, and from self-love. From it he learned to love suffering and to allow himself to be nailed to the cross with Christ, to die to the "animal man" and to the "reasoning man," in order to bring the "Godlike man" to life. Here, perhaps for the first time he met St. Augustine and St. Bernard, whose writings confirmed his own experiences and thus attracted him to "read" more of their works. He knew practically the entire book from memory and used expressions and examples from it in his works. Thus the *Mantelet* says, "that man, since he is always strongly inclined to sense-pleasures, needs to block their path with the hedges and thorns (of adversity)." John of St. Samson wrote in a similar vein, "we must block off all the avenues of our senses and of our sensuality with crosses."[11]

The works of all these writers formed the foundation of Brother John's spirituality. The period of formation probably covered the years 1595 to 1605 before his entrance into the Order. Did he have a spiritual guide at this time? There is no certain information that he had. It would seem that his wide reading and the grace of God sufficed for him. He had many disciples, but we can find no one who was his spiritual master. This may account for the great difference between him and other mystics of his time. His manner of expressing himself reflects not the contemporary masters of the spiritual life, but rather those of the previous centuries. When reading his works one thinks of him rather as a contemporary of Ruysbroeck than of St. Francis de Sales, St. Teresa of Avila, or St. John of the Cross. It seems that he grew to spiritual greatness alone. But in achieving this spiritual growth, he was deeply influenced by Pseudo-Denis, Tauler and especially Ruysbroeck and Harphius (or, Henry Herp).

In his written works he stresses the need of a spiritual director for all souls striving after perfection. And from Matthew Pinault we learn that about 1604-1605 two young men placed themselves under John's direction. They performed some charitable services like reading for him, taking him to hear sermons and, "they also went to the Sorbonne to seek advice concerning the difficulties experienced by John in prayer, for he received many great lights from God."[12] This however does not indicate that he had a spiritual master. Certainly such a situation is not unheard of. Did St. John of the Cross, for example, have a spiritual master, or St. Therese, the Little Flower? In religious life, Brother John often spoke with theologians and fervent men of prayer. At Dol there was Father Louis de Cenis, and Bishop Anthony de Revol. At Rennes he was in constant touch with the Carmelites who were key men in the Reform. With them and with visiting theologians he discussed mystical questions. But John did not submit his personal interior life to discussion, for the members of the community declared that he "made himself known with difficulty."

DOCTRINE AND TEACHING

The spiritual doctrine of John of St. Samson was not fully developed before his entrance into the Order, although he appears to have reached the highest stage of the mystical life by that time. His doctrine continued to develop during the years he lived at the Carmelite monastery of Rennes. There it was deepened by experience, the reading of the Scriptures and the Fathers. It was tested through the direction of his many disciples, and sifted by profound discussions with learned theologians and holy souls well versed in mental prayer and the ways of the spiritual life, like Dominic of St. Albert.

We must not forget that this great Carmelite mystic was blind. So the process of doctrinal synthesis was different from that of a John of the Cross. He had to depend on readers who did not always read what he preferred nor for as long as he would wish, or even at a time when he found it suitable. He heard many sermons, both good and bad. His retentive memory absorbed everything. In leisure hours and hours of prayer his mind slowly assimilated this content. The ideas he absorbed were carefully checked against his own experiences. What he found to be similar to his interior life he retained and made his own. Thus his thought was formed on that of other spiritual writers only insofar as they confirmed and explained his inner experiences. Finally, he reached a stage of perfection when he passed beyond all of their teachings. If he belonged to any school, most certainly it was that of the Holy Spirit, for he was highly endowed with the gift of divine wisdom. What he read in the writings of other spiritual masters furnished him with the means of expressing his own experiences and convictions.

The language in many respects is similar to that of the Rhenish mystics, especially Ruysbroeck and Herp. Although he relied on their teachings, he also has his own originality. True, he uses their system and terminology to express his own mystical experiences, but on a number of subjects he developed his own theory of the spiritual life and the soul's progress in it. A good example of this is his doctrine on "aspirative prayer." Here John develops the teaching of Henry Herp. Herp teaches that prayer of aspiration attains its goal when the lower faculties of the soul (appetite of desire, irascible appetite, and lower reason) have reached simplication and introversion.[13] Once this is accomplished, aspiration becomes superfluous, because the lower faculties have transferred their directing role to the higher faculties of intellect and will in the soul's ascent to God. Thus, according to Herp, aspirative prayer no longer appears in the higher degrees of the spiritual life. According to John of St. Samson the "introversion of the lower faculties is only the first stage of this prayer. It reaches its full development in the illuminative way. It is the means par-excellence for arriving at union with God, because it helps to strengthen and purify love and also to perfect the introversion of the higher faculties of the soul. As long as the process of introversion has not been fully achieved and as long as the soul feels there is a distinction between itself and God, aspirative prayer remains active. Thus, John prolongs the practice of aspiration up to the most profound stage of the introversion of the soul's higher faculties: the depth of the soul. Besides other secondary additions and new practices which he adds, this fact alone suffices to give prayer of aspiration an entirely different character (role)."[14] Thus we see that John of St. Samson's doctrine is his own, born of his own inner experience and perfected by divine grace.

From the outset, as a person begins to travel the road of perfection, John demands conformity to Christ interiorly and exteriorly, also complete detachment and self-denial, or love of the cross. Recall his motto, "With Christ I am nailed to the cross." Father Donatien

aspiration, a strong desire to achieve something noble
introversion — to be interested in your own mental life then the
world around you.

writes, "He relished these mysterious words in a wonderful manner, believing that they were written for him, and engraved them so deeply on his heart that he made them his most cherished motto, and pronounced them as his last words many times before he died."[15] Further on, Father Donatien writes, "He was a perfect imitator of Jesus Christ, and all his life he had the most tender feelings of love for the cross, for suffering, for death. These three, he said, were really only one thing for the loving soul."[16] In order to pass from his own nothingness into the All of God, man must leave himself totally. Although he directs the soul to sublime heights, John of St. Samson always insists on discretion and moderation.

Father Donatien has written some beautiful thoughts on John's teaching concerning the imitation of Christ. The crucified Christ was stripped. Therefore the soul that seeks perfection must "nakedly follow the naked Christ." The crucified Christ was solitary. Solitude places us in the presence of God and clothes us with the truth. It ought to have more influence on the soul than on the body, and demands forgetfulness of self. In the beginning, it is true, solitude demands strict discipline, but for him "who is dead on the cross while yet living," solitude becomes "a paradise," for it is "the field of the combats of love."

The crucified Christ was sacrificed. In this condition he is the perfect model for religious. "I say that the religious state is a state of total detachment from self and created things by a complete transformation of the soul into God. To be a religious is to die and live only in God and for God to the complete consummation of flesh and blood in the fire of his love. It is to live in perfect and complete poverty of spirit which has several degrees and states. It demands that the soul live in the practice of love, entirely detached from all that belongs to the senses and even from that which belongs to the spirit. In general it ought to be detached from all in which one can seek repose and satisfaction whether directly or indirectly."[17]

Christ continues to be on the cross in the Eucharist in order to be united with souls, to nourish and assimilate them to himself, to transform them into a unique offering of love. "It is this same

Bread of the Angels which we have eaten and still eat, Bread which your love and goodness had kneaded by the tribulations of your life and of your sorrowful Passion, Bread baked and re-baked on the bloody altar of the Cross in all the intense ardors of the furnace of your love for the sake of men."[18]

Suffering thus leads to joy, death leads to life, because everything is done out of love. Love, "naked, simple and essential" introduces the soul into the repose of God. In this repose the soul is royally poor and free, it is no longer the soul that lives, but it is God who lives in it. Transformed in the fire of love, and consummated in its Object, the soul becomes divine by participation in the uncreated Essence. But love cannot cease to be active. It would no longer be love. Love's repose is not in idleness. The loss of the soul in God is not an identity with divine nature, union is not essential, for even in glory the creature will remain a creature.[19]

Some recent studies, especially the thorough study entitled *La Reforme des Carmes en France et Jean de St. Samson* by Dr. Suzanne Michel (Bouchereaux), maintain that the heart, of John of St. Samson's doctrine is Pauline. Though he does not expressly quote St. Paul, still his thought is evident on almost every page. It is presented as it was understood and lived by John. He made it his own. We must become spiritual, because we are to be transformed in God who is pure spirit. For this reason, the old man must die on the cross with Christ. Then, clothed with the risen Christ, our life will be hidden in God with Jesus Christ; we will live in him or rather, he will live in us. And finally, when the soul has been completely purified, we will be consumed in him and enter the repose of God, or "the divine repose in the state of perfection."[20]

As a mystical writer, Brother John is a commanding figure. One of the most beautiful works in mystical literature is his *Epithalamium of Love,* or *Bridal Song of Love,* quite orthodox yet daring and remarkable in its originality. There he reveals his own interior life in the far reaches of the mystical marriage, in terms of such intimacy that the reader is astonished at the boldness of the description. Yet he never errs or strays from the truth. Here we see all the folly of love for the divine Spouse, and the ineffable life of a soul that shares in the life of the Holy Trinity.[21]

As we read his writings we become convinced that we are here faced by a spiritual giant who speaks with authority and from experience on the most profound aspects of the spiritual life. Ordinarily, he conceals this experience, but at times he admits it with a humble simplicity. We must admit that there is some obscurity in the expression of his teaching. This is due to his physical blindness. As we penetrate more deeply into his thought, overlooking the somewhat awkward expression, we are rewarded by a profound insight into the life of the soul with God. His lack of order reminds us of St. Teresa of Avila who often digressed from the original subject, yet her digressions were as informative and inspiring as the original theme itself. So it is with John of St. Samson. His wish us to inflame the heart more than to instruct the mind.

When John writes for the good of souls, whether it be in his treatises or in his *Letters,* he combines firmness, even severity with gentleness. When he gives advice it is without a trace of human respect. When he teaches or instructs it is with assurance. "Whoever writes for posterity, must do so with freedom and according to the truth."[22] Having reached perfect union with God, he was conscious of his mission to instruct and guide souls in the way of perfection and union with God.

Here we might ask, What did contemporary theologians and spiritual experts think of John's writings? We are fortunate in possessing the written opinions of a number of such critics. Bishop Francis of Killala, Ireland, at that time exiled from his diocese because of religious persecution, writes these impressions:

> We testify that Brother John's Works are full of an altogether heavenly wisdom and of a very pure mystical theology. The reading of them has only confirmed us in the high esteem that we already have for their author. That is why we consider his Works most worthy of being given to the public, hoping that chosen souls will be encouraged by them to follow the ways of higher perfection (July 16, 1658).[23]

The Dominican theologian and preacher, Florent Ranciat writes:

While reading *The True Spirit of Carmel*, I discovered the reason why this great religious has been blind from the cradle, namely, that the miraculous works of God might be manifested in him and that we might see how admirable he is in his saints. It is quite useless and very immaterial to have eyes when we desire only to be enlightened by the light of paradise, and wish to see only the beauties of the Divinity.

To me this work appears to be more the product of an angel than of a man. It seems that God wished its author to be blind in order to show that the senses have no part in the wisdom which was communicated to him after the manner of the angels by a divine infusion. The style is as divine as his thoughts, and as exalted as the doctrine which it expresses.[24]

From the Diocese of St. Brieuc we have the following appraisal from the official theologian of the diocese, Father John Baptist Noulleau:

No one is better suited for mystical theology than a blind person; and nothing is better suited to a blind person than mystical theology. We see both in this good Brother, blind almost from his birth. He was so enlightened in this kind of theology which is the most sublime and most eminent, that we can say he was only blind in order to see more clearly in it. His physical blindness withdrew him from created objects. Thus withdrawn from creatures he advanced toward God, and advanced so close to him that the brightness of his infinite Majesty which he could not endure in the abyss of his light caused a second blindness. The first was natural, the second was mystical. By the first he did not see creatures at all. By the second he saw God in such a great light that it became darkness for him. (Rennes, June 27, 1651).[25]

The same theologian also penned a brief evaluation of John's complete works.

All the Works of the Ven. Brother John of St. Samson manifest the same spirit. He is always on fire with love. In few authors does the spirit of grace have more influence over them than the spirit of nature. But where the former reigns as it does in this author and in all his works, everything is uniform, of the same elevation, the same solidity, of the same grace and most orthodox (July 1, 1655).[26]

A final testimony from one of the most renowned members of the Reform of Touraine, Leo of St. John.

> Never has there been an ignorant person so learned, a lay brother so filled with the science of the saints, or a blind person so enlightened. I consider it one of the mercies of God to have had the happiness of knowing this holy Theodidact (i.e., *one taught by God*) intimately, of serving as secretary to this rare author in my early years, and of learning the little that I know of the ways of grace from the lessons and examples of this great Master of the spiritual life. In order to show the value of his *Contemplations* I content myself with saying to all truly devout souls, "Taste and you will see!" (Paris, Monastery of the Most Blessed Sacrament, Feb. 2, 1654).[27]

Among his written works can be found even regulations for conducting the Reform. Where the Reform was concerned his judgment was sound and his observations were full of wisdom. John definitely helped to direct the Reform. For example, he suggested the names of the directors of the houses for the young professed, the measures to be followed in regulating studies while at the same time preserving interior recollection. Dominic of St. Albert, who became Vicar Provincial in 1630, did nothing without his counsel. John wrote a special treatise entitled the *"Direction of Novices,"*[28] in order to instill the principles of the Reform into the young religious from the very beginning of religious life. He wrote another treatise on the choice of superiors, *"Lights and Rules of Discretion for Superiors."*[29] Brother John wishes them to be "learned, enlightened, virtuous, perfectly charitable."[30] Quite minutely he lists their good qualities and their faults, and then says, "Therefore, examine your conscience, for it must render an account to God for so many sins committed through laxity, negligence and omission of the good which you ought to have done."[31] He insists on a wise distribution of material things for the good government of a monastery and for the peace of the religious living in it. He censures stingy superiors who allow their religious to want for even the necessities of life. Quite frankly he blames superiors who employ their religious "inside and outside the monastery in such a way

as to overburden them with continual labors until they crack under
the burden."[32] Nor is he any the less severe with those who prefer
rather to build new edifices than to reform their religious, or who
are always crying about poverty, but "forget about it where their
stomach is concerned," who give themselves up to the "ways of
beggars" in order to obtain money.[33]

Since he had willing secretaries, he used them to write down
the many canticles or hymns which he composed. A number of
these deal with the Incarnation, the Passion of Jesus, the Blessed
Virgin, St. Joseph, St. John the Baptist, St. Mary Magdalen, etc.
They are very long, running into 140 verses in a number of in-
stances. The thought in them is quite beautiful and sometimes the
expression, but their poetic value is negligible.[34] He would often
sing these canticles, accompanying himself on a stringed instrument
in his cell in order to become more recollected in God. Afterwards,
fearing that he had disturbed his brethren in neighboring rooms,
he would knock at their door and beg their pardon.

In his *Letters* John's doctrine takes on a personal warmth not
evident in his large treatises, except perhaps in his *Soliloquies* and
Contemplations. Although he dictated a great many letters, only
ninety of them have been preserved, covering a period of ten years,
1626-1636. In these *Letters* we see the true personality of John
of St. Samson. He is affectionate, familiar and simple, yet at times
exacting with his friends, for he always has their spiritual advance-
ment at heart. If they show signs of lagging, he gently and affection-
ately reproaches them. At times he will speak of a fond memory
once shared with his correspondent. Then he sends the present of
a medal, or of a rosary which will bind their friendship more
closely. He is really interested in all that concerns his friends:
their health, studies, the burden of their duties, the needs of their
old age.

To one of his correspondents he writes, "They say you are
threatened with a long and troublesome illness, like the one with
which I have been greatly afflicted. Use every means according
to prudence and sound reason to get rid of it, in as much as God
wishes it so. He wants us to live, as much as possible, in complete
health; in sickness, as much as he desires, and to die when it is

necessary."[35] He encourages his old friend M. Douet to continue to play the lute. And he does not hesitate to dispense advice to his dear friend, the Rector of Roz, on his private affairs, such as the choice of a successor in his parish.

However, the reader would be disappointed in reading the published edition of John's *Letters* edited by Father Donatien. The editor was content merely to preserve the doctrine, and ruthlessly pruned out place, date, destination, introduction and ending of the *Letters*. Sometimes he even joined two letters into one, cutting out lines or changing embarrassing words. Thus we fail to get a true picture of the warm, friendly personality of John of St. Samson.

STYLE

John of St. Samson's style leaves something to be desired. In the composition of his books there is a vague logical outline or schema, but he has no sooner begun to dictate than there is a digression. These digressions, however, are not tiresome. They are in fact instructive. Still they are excessive. On the other hand, to try to put order into this thought by eliminating all digressions would be to destroy his spontaneity and originality. When he dictated, his thoughts and ideas came in great profusion. The problem then was to organize them into a logical order. In this he failed. Although he possessed a rich and very descriptive vocabulary, he was still wanting in the art of speech.

Under obedience he set himself to the task of composing instructions for the novices and his many disciples. He began with a clearly defined subject and presently by association, one idea called up another. Soon he digressed from the original thought. On becoming aware of this, he would quite calmly say, "Let us return to our first line of thought." At times he would make express reference to this difficulty, "From all that, one can see what I wanted to say in all this disorder, and particularly in this passage" (cf. Sentences, fol. 76).[36] His first concern was to instruct souls in the ways of God and to guide them to that much desired union of love with the divine Spouse, Jesus Christ. He was quite conscious that he was an instrument of divine Wisdom, and often was under its manifest influence, which he was unable to conceal. What exterior defects are evident in his writings are due to his blindness. Had he been able to re-read them he would have re-written them. But he did not fail in his purpose. His writings are a spiritual gold mine.

Being blind from his earliest years, his thinking is ordinarily quite abstract and devoid of images. His ideas are abundant and full of wisdom, but since he frequently writes about the most profound aspects of the interior life, his style is somewhat heavy. In spite of this it seldom loses its conversational tone. The high level of his thought, the ease and simplicity, the freedom and vigor with which he expresses it, make the reading of his Works very rewarding. His ideas are developed slowly. They are presented with authority and undoubted experience. Certain thoughts occur frequently in varied form, such as the joys of divine love, the union of the soul with the Spouse, detachment, love of the cross, constant mortification of self-love in all its manifestations, prayer of aspiration, etc. He knows as a spiritual director, that the soul tends to forget essential practices, and that they must be constantly repeated if they are to be effective in the soul's interior life. His one purpose in all this is to insist upon that mortification of self which leads to the death of the "old man" so that the soul may be transformed in the image of Christ.

The reader will also notice an obscurity of expression that is in part due to the nature of the subject, the mystical life. And at times John deliberately cultivates an obscure style. He writes, "If I am obscure in places it is because I have considered it unsuitable to be open in these matters. For I am convinced that everyone who wishes to be spiritual will see and understand (*what I say*) without difficulty."[37] The Carmelite Master of Rennes wished to preserve the secret of the divine King from curious eyes. Yet he did not avoid describing the most elevated mystical states, in spite of his lack of formal scholastic training. Where St. John of the Cross refused to describe the exalted state of the transforming union at any length, John of St. Samson did not hesitate to say that even in this state there was a beginner's stage, an advanced stage and finally, a perfect stage. But the terminology of the two mystical writers is quite different. St. John of the Cross uses the terminology of the scholastics, whereas John of St. Samson uses a terminology that was already archaic at the time he composed his mystical Works. The reader at once thinks that he is reading a work written by mystics of the Flemish school, like Ruysbroeck and Herp, or by a Rhenish mystic like Tauler. What adds to the obscurity of his style is that Brother John does not mean exactly the same thing as Ruysbroeck by such terms as 'super-essential,' 'naked and essential love,' 'supereminent,' 'contemplation,' etc. He gives them a meaning peculiar to his own experience. But the accusation that John did not understand Ruysbroeck's system is not true. John "assimilated perfectly the difficult ontological system of Ruysbroeck and Herp with its terms and descriptions which are so obscure to the uninitiated. He made their terminology a part of his own mystical experiences."[38] The student of mysticism will have no difficulty in recognizing the origin of John's doctrine when reading his writings.

In spite of himself the blind Master is verbose and his thought becomes involved. He relies on abstract and unadorned description of mystical experiences, ordinarily avoiding comparisons and analogies. When he does use figures of speech they are not original. But because they are assimilated to his spirituality, they fit in quite naturally with his description and add charm to his vigorous thought. Thus he speaks of the "sun of love that makes the land of the heart of man fruitful." The vices are called "weeds." Humility is compared to a tree planted in the heart of the good and produces all the virtues. Love is compared to an archer. He often speaks of the game of love, the palace of love, the stairway of love. The absence of the divine Spouse is compared to the rigors of winter. The soul lost in God is in its center and repose, like the fish that has plunged into the flowing water which is its proper element. He compares the soul that yearns to 'absorb' God to the fish that "wishes to swallow the sea and is itself swallowed by the sea." Speaking of those who possess a counterfeit spirituality, John of St. Samson says that they appear to be as radiant "as the phoenix," but in the end turn out to be "black crows." At times the musician in him appears in his comparisons ; e.g. "human affairs are made up of order and disorder, which in itself produces a harmony composed of discordant chords."[39]

In the original and unabridged Works the style of John of St. Samson flows easily and is often lyrical, especially when he speaks of divine love and the mystical union of the soul with God. The actual number of subjects treated are not many, and can readily be reduced to the essential themes of the spiritual life. But his great power of analysis enables him to consider these subjects from many aspects and to go into great detail, especially on the virtues, contemplation, love of God, mortification, prayer, the effect of grace and of self-love in the soul.

LIST OF WORKS

The Works of John of St. Samson were published in part by Father Donatien of St. Nicholas in 1650. The large edition of his Works in two Tomes appeared in 1658 at Rennes, edited by Father Donatien and published by P. Coupard. Each page has a double column of print, and each column is equivalent to a page of our modern book. This by no means covers all that he wrote, for much of it still remains in manuscript form. Here we present only a list of his printed works. The French titles have been translated for the benefit of the average reader. To date, only one small edition of his *Maxims* have been translated into English.

TOME I

A Brief Summary of the Life of John of St. Samson by Donatien of St. Nicholas, O. Carm., pp. 1-60.

The True Spirit of Carmel, pp. 1-133.

The Mystical Cabinet (for more enlightened souls), pp. 135-224.

Mirror of Conscience (for advanced souls), pp. 224-280.

Rules for Conversation, pp. 280-301.

Mirror and Flames of Divine Love (intended to dispose the soul to love God for Himself), pp. 302-336.

Soliloquies (Interior, affectionate and familiar conversations of the soul with God), pp. 337-384.

Contemplations on the Mysterious Effects of Divine Love, pp. 385-528.

Meditations for a Ten Day Retreat, pp. 529-586.

Lights and Rules of Discretion for Superiors, pp. 587-616.

TOME II

Collection of Spiritual Letters, pp. 617-680.

Holy Simplicity, pp. 681-744.

Man's Withdrawal from God and His Return to Him (concerns the mystical life), pp. 745-781.

The Death of the Saints, or *How to Suffer and Die Holily,"* pp. 782-846.

Observations on the Carmelite Rule, pp. 847-892.

Direction of Novices, pp. 892-968.

Various Treatises, pp. 969-1044.

1. *Perfection and Ruin of Religious Life*
2. *When One May Refuse or Resign the Office of Superior*
3. *Thoughts on Establishing and Maintaining Reforms*
4. *Holy Communion*
5. *Diabolic Possession* (intended for an exorcist)
6. *Excellence and Exalted Dignity of the Priesthood*
7. *Christian Fortitude*

Mystical Poems:

1. *Ingratitude of the Sinner Towards God*
2. *The Triumph of the Cross*
3. *Grandeurs and Merits of Our Lady*
4. *In Honor of St. Joseph, Spouse of the Blessed Virgin Mary*
5. *Spouses of the Cross are Blessed*
6. *Of the Highest and Purest Renunciation*
7. *Loving Sorrows of St. Mary Magdalen at the Sepulchre of Jesus*

1 Oeuvres de Jean de S. Samson, t. I, p. 65.

2. Ms. Joseph, p. 29.

3. Op. cit., p. 133.

4. Ms. Joseph, p. 33; also Bouchereaux, op. cit., p. 159.

5. Oeuvres de Jean de S. Samson, t. II, Letter XV to Father Valentin, p. 629.

6. Bouchereaux, op. cit., p. 160.

7. Oeuvres de Jean de S. Samson, t. I, p. 595.

8. Ms. Joseph, p. 131.

9. Janssen, op. cit., p. 232; also Oeuvres de Jean de S. Samson, t. II, p. 902, col. 1, C.

10. Bouchereaux, op. cit., p. 162.

11. Oeuvres de Jean de S. Samson, t. I, p. 16.

12. Ms. Joseph, p. 25.

13. Introversion is a turning inward, a concentration of the soul's interior powers upon God Who dwells in its center. In modern psychology the lower faculties of the soul would here include imagination and sense memory, besides the emotions (passions), and reason as applied to sense objects.

14. Janssen, op. cit., p. 242-243.

15. Op. cit., p. 4.

16. Ibid., p. 112.

17. Oeuvres de Jean de S. Samson, t. I, p. 7.

18. Ibid., Contemplations XVIII, t. I, p. 454.

19. The four paragraphs above may be found in "Diréctions pour la vie intérieure" by Jean de St. Samson, collected and presented by Dr. Suzanne Bouchereaux, Paris, 1948; p. 18-20.

20. Heb. 4, 10; also, Oeuvres de Jean de S. Samson; True Spirit of Carmel, t. I, p. 128; cf. Bouchereaux, op. cit., p. 268-269.

21. L'Epithalame de Jean de Saint-Samson by Susanne Michel (Bouchereaux) in Carmelus, vol. I, 1954, p. 72-110; also the complete text of the Epithalame, p. 158-175. It is an excellent study.

22. Oeuvres de Jean de S. Samson: Observations on the Carmelite Rule, t. II, p. 850.

23. Ibid., t. I, p. 61.

24. Ibid., t. I, p. 63.

25. Ibid., t. I, p. 63-64.

26. Ibid., I, p. 64.

27. Ibid., t. I, p. 65.

28. Ibid., t. II, pp. 892-968.

29. **Ibid.**, t. I, p. 587-616.
30. **Ibid.**, t. I, p. 590.
31. **Ibid.**, t. I, p. 616.
32. **Ibid.**, t. I, p. 595.
33. **Ibid.**, t. I, p. 600.
34. Most of these canticles, poems, etc. remain in manuscript form.
35. **Oeuvres de Jean de S. Samson: Letter XXVI**, t. II, pp. 636-637.
36. Bouchereaux, **op. cit.**, p. 164.
37. "Directions pour la vie intérieure," by John of St. Samson, edited by Dr. Susanne Bouchereaux; cf. Introduction, p. 25, footnote, n. 1.
38. Janssen, **op. cit.**, p. 234.
39. **Oeuvres de Jean de S. Samson: True Spirit of Carmel.** t. I, p. 33.

PART II

A SELECTION OF HIS WRITINGS

CHAPTER I

PRAYER

VOCAL PRAYER

(*Psalms*)   When you recite the Psalms, do not be too concerned about getting the meaning of the texts, unless it is disclosed to you. Then it will urge you toward God like a sharp spur as it presents the picture of his many wonders to you. At such a time you must be content to let your mind and heart simply see and feel while they are inspired with holy sentiments. Look at God with a simple gaze, and prefer this to any devout and stimulating converse.

Finally, you must be more concerned about having a simple attention and intention, and an affection that regards God simply and essentially, rather than having a complete understanding (*of the text*). Those, who have some experience in divine Wisdom, know this truth well, and willingly surrender reason to it. But the purely learned and others act quite differently on such occasions. This practice, however, is the way to recite the Psalms in a holy manner. For we ought to pay more attention to God and our simple, savorous inclination toward him than to the most profound and richest meanings searched out with effort. By the former we adhere to God nakedly and purely. By the latter we encounter distraction and division.

MENTAL PRAYER

(*Posture*)   The posture we assume while praying is not important, as long as it is becoming. We must avoid overburdening the spirit under the weight of the body. If possible, we should keep the soul completely abstracted from the feeling of the body, so that, being thus strengthened, we may be able to maintain an attention that is alert and actual during our prayers. We may also pray while walking without acting contrary to perfection, as long as we walk slowly and quietly. By this means many can more easily maintain a profound attention.

(*Advice given to an advanced soul*)   As far as the body is concerned, assume the posture that will give you the least trouble. For example, if, instead of kneeling, you find it better to stand, then remain standing; or, if a sitting position is better, then be seated. Spend part of your time in one position, then change to another if it suits you. This rule is very necessary because of the great affinity that exists between the soul and the body. If the body is overwhelmed with sufferings and the imagination is crowded with diverse images, the soul will not be very tranquil or alert in its activity. Still, in the case of advanced souls who do not desire these distractions, the soul is always profoundly absorbed in God.

(*Meditation*)   Meditation has a number of degrees. When the soul has gained facility in it, it is called *prayer*. This is one degree. Another is the cessation from prolonged, lively and affective discourse. This is followed by spontaneous affection while the soul is still in itself (*and not in God*). Afterwards God gives the understanding, will and memory a strong attraction. Under the influence of this sweet attraction, the soul contemplates him who draws it and keeps it suspended in himself. Thus it remains completely recollected in all its faculties, filled with delights and most secret lights which God produces in it. All these exercises are an exalted and excellent form of contemplation.

   On such an occasion God manifests himself so abundantly and reveals so many marvelous secrets that the soul finds it impossible to explain what it has seen or felt. Within its soul it is completely and ineffably liquified in the love of its dear Spouse.

(*Outside the time for mental prayer*)   Recall, as much as possible, the affections you made in it (i.e. mental prayer), and renew them frequently, so that when circumstances demand it, you will easily be able to back up your desires with good works. We all know that love cannot be idle in a soul. If it is idle, it no longer deserves the title of love. Then it becomes negligence, laziness, and infidelity. But the soul that possesses this love constantly unites itself to its Spouse by frequent renewals of its love in its actions and affections. It never permits the vain images of creatures to invade the domain of God within it.

Since your meditation in the morning is on the most bitter Passion of our dear Savior, in the evening, it would be good, for fear of being bored, to meditate on some sentences taken from Holy Scripture, such as, "Man, when he was in honor, did not understand," etc. (Ps 48:21). "Precious in the sight of the Lord is the death of his saints." "Christ was obedient for us even unto death." "The Lord has chastened me, chastened me indeed" (Ps 117: 118). Select verses that are ardent and meaningful. At the most, spend only an hour in prayer, and then pray in such a way that you prefer rather to listen than to speak. Be careful not to overwork your understanding. On the other hand, do not neglect it or leave it idle. After the understanding has discovered the prize, it should give an equal share of the prize to the will. In this way, these two faculties will not claim the riches of the Spirit to the prejudice of each other.

When you are conscious of being truly and abundantly visited by the Spirit of God, consider yourself unworthy of his visit. And if the Divine Spirit continues his action in you, showering you with divine delights so that you cannot doubt the real presence of your Spouse within you, return this gift to him. But do so without refusing it, since he has deigned to give it to you. During his visit, do nothing with your spirit until he is gone. Then become occupied in him as before, by using the efficacious light which he has left in you. Thus you will be able to fly to him quite simply and easily with the wings of an ardent love, guided by very simple and subtle glances. In books dealing with the subject, you will find aspirations of all kinds which are quite suitable for beginning this practice.

The will is the master in all this (i.e. *in making acts of love, conversions to God and the simple intention to do and endure all things in God,* etc.). And it is the will that must apply itself completely and always in this holy exercise. Now, what we said about the obligation of the understanding and the will to remain active is to be understood only of those who meditate. Even here the understanding must cease its activity once the will is sufficiently inflamed. This is so important that many, who are ignorant of it, remain in themselves almost all their life. They are tepid and stagnant, because they rely only upon the activity of their intellect. This faculty knows only how to speculate, for it has a natural curiosity to understand what it doesn't know. On the other hand, once the will has received the illumination of the understanding, it becomes ardently inflamed with love for its Object, and for as long a time as necessity demands.

This is the way these souls should conduct themselves in prayer. They ought to conclude it with heartfelt and ardent affections. Indeed, if they could always pray in this way, it would be prayer well done. For to tell the truth, the union of our soul with God is only accomplished by an active will inflamed with love for its divine Object. From this we may safely conclude that this holy practice is an exercise intended for the will. If the will is wanting in it, then the actual reformation of the soul and its transformation in God will also be wanting. Therefore, we must resolve to be continually active in forming profound, heartfelt laments and burning sighs.

If you do this faithfully, you will find yourself in time at the peak of high perfection, in union with God himself. You will find it easy to form the simpler and more exalted aspirations, which raise the soul to the highest perfection of transforming love, from God to God himself. Thus, the paradise of God in the soul and of the soul in God consists in the continual practice of this holy exercise. For what should we be doing every moment of our life, if not expiring completely in God, through the power of his love.

(Ways of approaching God)   The active life ought to be exercised more with the spirit than with the body. When such a practice becomes a habit, the spirit is touched by God in a series of such experiences. Thus he draws it out of itself and unites it to his

divine Majesty by frequent turnings to it. The sweetness experienced at this time makes it easy for the soul to pray. However, this is not discovered soon enough, because there are diverse entrances depending on the diversity of natures and the disposition of the soul. Those who are more remote, meditate on the horror of sin simply and lovingly, without using the scholastic method of speculation. Others, however, meditate on subjects that are more concerned with love than with fear. But this depends on simplicity of heart, which develops the soul's aptitude for God's touches.

Natures that are too lively and animal,[1] are fit only for vocal prayer. During the time for mental prayer they should be advised to practice with subjects that are pleasant and easy to digest, arranged in such a way that they may be able to pray without weariness. Outside the time of prayer, they should often form ejaculatory prayers in order to preserve some feeling for God. This practice, followed according to the direction given novices and professed, will gradually elevate them to the point where they will be able to turn to God quite easily and remain occupied with him without encountering interior obstacles.

The subject of ordinary mental prayer ought to be the holy Passion of our Savior. It is an inexhaustible and very fruitful book, simply and vividly revealing his eternal and infinite love for his elect and well-beloved children. According to St. Bernard, there are three ways of penetrating this profound subject: 1) The *work* itself, that is to say, the vehemence of the infinite sorrows of Jesus Christ, in his Soul and Body. It is a fathomless sea. 2) The *manner,* that is, the profound and most fervent humility with which the eternal Word, clothed in our humanity, humbled himself even to an ignominious death on the cross. In this he is an admirable mirror, reflecting the most heroic virtues, with an infinite fervor of spirit. Thus, by his example, we are encouraged to live and suffer in the thought of him alone, who accomplished these prodigies among men out of love for them. 3) The *cause,* which clearly shows the eternal and infinite love out of which we have been created, and admirably re-created through the Passion of a God made man. He suffered in the greatest extreme for the excesses of men, in order to convert them by the power of his love, and to draw them from

the love of themselves to love of him Who is infinite love. In this
way he wanted them to be able to share his own divine nature.

The *first* of these methods is for beginners; the *second,* for those
who are advanced; and the *third,* for those who seek perfection
with all their strength, and with a sincere and simple love, besides
the earnest practice of the virtues exercised with the same kind
of love.

*(Concerning souls who undertake spiritual exercises out of self-love
and because of a natural pleasure they find in them.)* Even though
these persons eagerly devote themselves to the study of the most
profound aspects of the interior life, they are still not suited for it.
For, when the depth of the soul is full of confusion and conflict,
it is directly opposed to the virtues. Hence it is unfit not only for
the interior life, but even for mental prayer. Such souls can only
be introduced to the lowest and easiest spiritual practices. Actually,
they are fit only for external things. At the most, they might undertake the practice of *mixed prayer* which is both vocal and mental.

Those who spend a great deal of time in prayer and yet derive
no profit from it, are like weak mountaineers who force themselves
to climb the sheer side of a high mountain. They are so weak that
they fall back at every step. Their work is almost fruitless, because
they do not want to give up their old habits. True, they have
desires enough, and speak a great deal about the virtues. But, they
are full of self-love, and when it is a question of dying to it and
the attachments born of it, they do not even know where to begin.
Indeed, they hardly even know what external perfection is.

(Dryness) If you are tempted either by self-love or by the devil
to quit prayer because of aridity or dryness, do not do so. Examine
this state to see if there is something in it that is due to your own
fault. If there is nothing in it that can be laid to your blame, then
remain in the divine Presence, and be attentive to God, trusting in
him for the grace to persevere in this exercise. But if there is something for which you are to blame, ask pardon for it, and correct it.
Then you will always be equally happy, whether you have sensible

consolations or not. In this state of privation, the divine Majesty tests the fidelity of his lovers to see if they will rest in him alone, for he is infinitely different from his gifts. Still, in this time of desolation, you may have recourse to brief ejaculatory prayer, unless some other subject offers itself. In that case you might talk with God about it until the end of prayer. Always conclude it with requests for your spiritual and corporal needs and those of your neighbor. And add humble acts of thanksgiving for the favors received from God, both in the present as well as in the course of your whole life.

Spiritual directors should carefully guard those who are ready for converse with God from over-working their faculties. In time of abundant consolation, they are inclined to be too active. There is even greater danger of this in time of dryness and abandonment. Therefore, in the spiritual state of ease and abundance, they must not force themselves to withdraw into their soul, because God is already drawing them quite skillfully by his secret attraction. It is sufficient if they act gently and moderately, withdrawing from self while drawing close to God.

But when they are not secretly drawn by God by means of lights and devout feelings, they must occupy themselves moderately in reading or in some other activity in order to find suitable material for dilating their prayer. And as for distractions, desolation, aridity and darkness, they should not be unduly alarmed over them. However, they should adopt certain means and practices. For example, some strive to return to God by the path of knowledge, a means they had used in the past. Thus, little by little, they excite the will and arouse some feeling for their subject. They manage quite well. Attention to self and a little bit of courage are necessary to avoid being troubled and wearied at seeing oneself isolated and left wandering from one subject to another, from one thought to another. Others continually think of their misery, which is not entirely wrong. But nature eventually becomes fed up with it, because this kind of thinking is too selfish. It is depressing and throws the soul back entirely upon itself. The soul rarely succeeds in attaining its good desires by this means, because, in the long run, nature becomes weary of such reflections. Sometimes it is unconsciously weary even of itself. Occasionally this method seems to be quite suited for certain souls, especially those who are somewhat lazy.

When the soul feels hindered in its power to act and is in such darkness that, when it wants to think of something good, it is like being in hell, then it must try to enkindle itself by reciting some very affective vocal prayer. It should continue this for some time with an earnest but moderate effort, until the heart and interior sense faculties are inflamed. Thus, the faculties will be moved to assimilate the considerations, which at one time wearied them, and the affections, which it launches toward God either vocally or directly from the heart. Those who can use these means will find them very helpful, not only for returning to their customary activity, but also, as it were, for urging God to communicate himself to the soul by his secret and subtle irradiations.[2] He will finally make the darkness and aridity vanish and enable the soul to perceive his sweet presence and efficacious light. Thus will he reward the soul for having persevered and lovingly grieved in the time of his absence. And the past will vanish and be changed in the sweetness and delight of a new and unexpected paradise.

From all this we can see how important it is to have wise and constant direction from beginning to end of the spiritual life, especially in the painful states of suffering and destitution. For all these things are the spiritual keys to life and death. If the soul is so full of misery and confusion, and so devoid of any desire to exert itself that it cannot possibly stir itself, then it must suffer with patience and resignation, and as calmly as possible. Let it surrender itself to God as a pure holocaust of love, by doing his divine will in its actions, sufferings and death, both for time and eternity.

But the difficulty is that, in these very painful languors, withdrawals and suspensions, the soul is strongly tempted to impatience, and thinks it is in a kind of hell. It sees its faculties laid open to innumerable violent thoughts and temptations coming one after another. Moreover, its director cannot remove them by any kind of reasoning, no matter how convincing it may be. Such explanations reach only the senses and the exterior. Often enough the soul is even more afflicted after such conversation than if nothing at all were

said to it. Now it is here that the soul inevitably fails in fidelity
when it is still new in the practice of prayer. Instead of rising above
its afflictions to God, it thinks only of itself. Thus it shows quite
clearly that it does not want to rise above itself, nor does it want
to be deprived of the sensible influence of the divine action which
draws, dilates and illumines its sense faculties. Formerly, it experienced and understood things of great import in knowledge and
light. Now, all that is forgotten and completely lost. The soul is
all alone and harassed by a thousand anxieties which penetrate its
inmost being. This state makes it as sorrowful as its former state
made it ardent, eager and fervent.

After being caressed for some time, the first withdrawal of God
from the soul is very painful. It is almost impossible to bear, if the
soul has no experience, and doesn't have enough strength and virtue.
For it will easily give up the combat and leave the field, unless
it is secretly assisted by God and very carefully guided by a good
director, who is well versed in this matter. He should know everything that happens to the soul on these occasions.

We must not follow the advice of those who say that, in this
very painful and wearisome state, beginners should not look for
consolation in creatures or in the reading of good books. For, at this
time the soul is doing a great deal simply by standing before God
as a victim, exposed to all the blows and attacks of nature as it is
tossed about by violent passions and temptations both from itself
as well as from the devils. It is too early to withdraw these persons
from the senses and from consolation, because they are absolutely
necessary for them in these new experiences. Therefore, they should
take advantage of them in so far as they can do so lawfully. To act
otherwise would be to force them to live, as it were, on air, in other
words, to do the impossible.

Actually, during these sufferings and withdrawals, directors must
distract these souls, and by no means leave them alone or solitary.
They should be employed in performing external tasks as much as
possible, tasks which are sufficiently diverting and require all their
attention to be done well. During and after the performance of
such tasks, the director should often visit them and encourage them
to practice solid virtue. He should also try to develop in them a

certain facility in dealing with intellectual subjects and in using devout considerations meant to transform the will by means of the affections which they arouse in the soul. This point is very important. Furthermore, the subjects must often be varied so as not to create disgust. Brief reflections, simple and easy to grasp, should be given them already developed. In this way they will be able to understand at least some part of them and put them into practice. Again, the director should allow them to read as much as they wish about such matters. But they must not be forced, otherwise they will develop an aversion for prayer and spiritual converse. In that case he would be doing them great harm. Hence, he ought to leave them free to act, and avoid urging them too much. Nor should he make them weary of what actually ought to be a remedy. Moreover, souls in this state should be very careful not to utter loud complaints to God, when they see that their faculties are suspended in their activity. Such conduct would only exhaust them and draw them up completely, unless they were already in that condition. In that case their state would be even worse, for, without common sense, they would become mentally unbalanced. Such an evil, if it is not forestalled right from the beginning by the prudence and skill of the director, is dangerous and incurable.

Therefore, from the very beginning, the director, with his enlightenment, should give full attention to the task of gaining a thorough knowledge of the souls under his direction. He should find out what path they are following, what subjects they use, what motives influence them directly or indirectly. He should know what acts they perform, and whether they are purely natural. Then too he should discover what inclination they have for introversion[3] and converse with God, what reflections they make when they are in darkness and why; their most secret and hidden thoughts, and many other similar things. He ought likewise to make a note of their desires by checking their inclinations. This can be done by observing their reactions. These will be revealed quite clearly, either freely and with the approval of their director, or by their attempts to conceal them. Thus directors should skillfully draw upon their own experience, in order to determine the interior state of the souls under their direction. In his procedure he should act in such a way that he doesn't seem to be making an investigation, being as pleasant about it as possible.

(*Distractions: Advanced souls*)   As for subtle distractions, which we must often endure because of the excessive burden of the body, it is best to pay no attention to them. They are so subtle that the soul is very often not even aware of them. Besides, they do not influence the will in the slightest degree, because they do not withdraw it from its Object. And even though more lively and more sensible distractions come to annoy us, so that we don't seem to be perfectly attentive to God or to persevere in the state of death and total self-annihilation, still we are very often actually being faithful to these demands. But we do fail, if we allow ourselves to take delight in pleasant and attractive objects. Thus, imperceptibly, we become careless and fail to make the effort required to remain simple and tranquil.

In order to avoid the distraction of these sensible objects, we must turn for help to the subtle work of reason, but without doing anything with our faculties. And when the disturbance becomes more annoying, we should recollect ourselves, or better, annihilate these distractions, as it were, with one breath. We should follow this procedure as long as we feel unduly disturbed. However, it is not enough to annihilate such distractions by using a simple gaze and naked faith. We must also annihilate their acts by frequently recollecting ourselves. Thus, by means of a very simple and complete abstraction,[4] we shall avoid these distractions, and at the same time keep up a simple and alert attention. When we do this, we have nothing to fear.

These distractions very often come from the devils, who excite the imagination in diverse ways. Besides, this faculty is inclined to seek itself under spiritual pretexts. Often too, distractions come from our disordered nature. It is always good to confess them in general. For usually, we see that we have, more or less, failed by allowing ourselves to become attached to these delightful and alluring images. This faculty (*imagination*) is never satisfied, where its own good is concerned.

Whatever a person is in his life and natural desires, that

he will be in his prayer, mental as well as vocal. Even those, who serve God with courage and sincerity, are not exempt from distractions. And even if these distractions are of a spiritual nature, still they detract from the purity and beauty of their present offering, especially in their vocal prayers. If sincere souls have distractions, imagine the distractions of those who are entangled in a thousand disordered desires! However, the spiritual persons mentioned above are not plagued by distractions, if they are very skillful in leaving themselves, and, at the same time, eagerly strive to see and feel the infinite majesty of God. In the sweet and loving fervor of their prayers, they are poured out heart and soul before God, like a very fragrant perfume. Beginners and more mediocre souls are immediately distracted when they begin to pray either mentally or vocally. Still, they should not lose heart over this. For, since they are very displeased with such persistent and importunate distractions, they are as far from being hurt in their combat, as, on the other hand, they suffer a real martyrdom because of them. Their directors ought to reassure them on this point, and provide them with a good method for handling these distractions. We cannot sufficiently impress on them the importance of attention during prayer. For lack of it they are really miserable. They lie as though dead, or, at least, like one who is more wounded than in perfect health.

The answer to this problem lies in controlling our nature and animal appetites by habits of long standing. The holy attention required in prayer demands great purity of intention and desire as well as peace of mind and heart, and similar dispositions that are to be found only in a soul having long experience in the spiritual life. Consequently, where these dispositions are absent and where the animal life is in complete control, the heart is bound to be greatly agitated during prayer. It is like a sea furiously whipped by the winds. For such people, prayer is a painful whip, especially because they do not expect to merit anything by it. Although they suffer in it voluntarily, they endure frequent and violent whirlwinds of the heart. And when they return to their duty, they suffer new torments through grievous remorse of conscience over their miserable and corrupt life. They see that sincere souls are united to God with all their heart by the very same exercise that removes them far from him. And the worst part of it is, if things remain as they are, they will live and die in this sad state.

As for those who are entangled in this corrupt state, and neither see nor feel their miserable condition, they are the worst of this unfortunate class. When they have recited a great many prayers with countless distractions, they consider themselves pardoned before God. This fact amazes me. And I am even more amazed at the fact that ordinary men neither see nor feel anything of this. Undoubtedly, this misfortune is due to their great blindness, a blindness that will remain with them until their death, because they do not want to know it. Even though the writings of the saints make them aware of their miserable state, they soon forget. And yet such knowledge only renders them more culpable before God. What security can they draw from such an unfortunate life! For God has no part in it, since their life and habits are so opposed to him. The two states are completely opposed to each other, the one being purely spiritual and the other very animal. If only they wanted to see this! If only this could be a mirror to make them see the countless evils that surround them! I wish it were a kind of medicinal antidote that they might take in order to make them vomit up all the deadly poison nature made them swallow. The Fathers and holy Doctors of the Church, both mystics and scholastics, agree on the truth of these matters.

If we are not on our guard, the devil and our own nature will disturb the soul during mental prayer and the recitation of the Divine Office. For example, they will suggest images of what we have already done, or desire to do whether it be good or bad. The best way to handle them is not to think about them. Or we can withdraw from them, as if we did not hear these buzzings, and continue our prayer in peace and tranquility. For, purely spiritual temptations and distractions must be resisted in a different manner than the distractions of the senses.

HIGHER FORMS OF PRAYER

(*Requirements*)   He who is simple according to these truths (viz.

that the way of love demands practice, not theory; that he should not pour himself out on external things in the active life, but should cultivate the intention of doing all for God alone,) very carefully avoids internal and external entanglement. He is far more concerned with the simple depth of his soul where he is completely recollected than with anything it might be able to produce for him, in order to keep him occupied. If, for the moment, he has some attractive interior occupation, it is God who provides it for reasons best known to him, and because it pleases him. And the soul, on its part, always remains steadfast in this interior state, in order to maintain a steady, naked and simple gaze upon its Object. Here the soul finds its repose and its life. Here it places all its good and its joy. And since there are neither forms nor images here, it carefully avoids the snare of being drawn away by these images, no matter how subtle they may be. In this state, it should desire nothing whatsoever, inasmuch as God is now simply seen and tasted. Wholly transfused in its spirit, the soul really possesses him as he is, by a simple and naked glance.

In this state, the soul delights in God alone in simplicity of repose beyond understanding. While it is thus wholly absorbed and occupied, the soul should be very careful not to leave this state, no matter how much pressure the senses may put on it for their relief. By their subtle influence, they persuade the soul to busy itself with the most lofty subjects, because they always want to see and feel something new. Actually they are only seeking their own secret and selfish satisfaction. But the prudent soul, once it is firmly fixed in contemplation and fidelity to its loving Object, patiently endures these subtle suggestions without harm, and refuses to encourage them in any way whatever. In fact they only serve as an incentive to the soul, urging it to maintain a more attentive and steady gaze upon its Object. On his part, God draws and transports the soul out of the senses and even out of itself into him, in whom it enjoys ineffable delights.

(*Caution: Warns the soul not to enter too soon into mystical prayer.*) No one is sufficiently disposed or fitted to enter into the supereminent[5] life, unless he is entirely deprived of his power to act, (*he is speaking of the purest and simplest form of the mystical life.*) Thus, it has some aptitude for the highest kind of mysticism. However, this must be true in every respect. For, as long as there remains even one degree of the ability to form an act of love, the soul does not have the required disposition to surrender itself completely as a victim to God. In order to take its first steps in the mystical and supereminent life the soul must lose and abandon itself completely.

Many, even learned mystics, seem to be unaware of this. In their writings they encourage souls (who are still too lively and active) to enter most eagerly into the arms of the infinite God, and abandon themselves to him for the purpose of being moved thereafter by him alone. But since they are still so full of life, and therefore have great unions and splendors to achieve and surpass regarding reciprocal love, they should not act in this way. Such a soul will often suffer grievous and infernal languors, since it is neither outside nor inside, for it has not yet experienced sweet, strong and burning mystical attractions. I say '*mystical*' purposely, because of the exalted eminence of these attractions. When the soul is really elevated to this state, it immediately receives delightful, secret, and glowing impressions of its loving Object.

When a soul has never enjoyed this experience, then certainly it has no disposition for such a supereminent attraction. Therefore, if it acts as though it enjoyed this favor, it only exposes itself to cruel languors and receives little fruit from it.

(*Stages of Prayer*)   The *first stage* of a person's return to God has a number of degrees, and a large circumference. As long as the soul depends on its own activity, it knows where it is going. But, because this kind of self activity seems to be purely human, it is not very good for rising above what is sensible. As long as the soul is not touched by God, it remains in itself, and feels more or less at ease in its own activity. During this time it is without light, taste or elevation.

(*Second stage*)   But in proportion as it is touched, elevated, enlightened and acted upon, it passes beyond the region of the senses and its own activity, and enters the region of the spirit. Here it is lost to itself and is more acted upon than acting. The soul is then raised above itself to a luminous and savoring knowledge of God's infinite grandeur and goodness, and of the nothingness of itself and of all things. These impressions give it a pleasant satisfaction which it gladly offers to God.

(*Third stage*)   Here, there is already a certain degree of simple contemplation which is above all feeling and affection. This occurs at the end of the active life, when it has reached its perfection. Gradually this exalted exercise becomes more perfect. Meanwhile, the soul is ennobled by marvelous infusions and illuminations. When such souls try to speak of their experience, they hardly know what to say, because their spirit is, as it were, suspended in this state and unable to express what it sees and feels. So they follow the spirit that attracts them. Now the more they profit by this practice, the more spiritual they become. In a corresponding degree they become more and more lost to sense-activity.

This form of prayer produces a gaze in the understanding which secretly ravishes the will. The soul is so occupied in following its attraction under very simple forms that all images by necessity remain outside. Under the influence of a simple and continual touch, the senses very willingly die to their own activity. But when they turn to something external, the spirit, by a quick movement, re-enters within, and turns away from it. Such souls look without drawing any image or form to themselves, because they are entirely governed by the spirit which quickly moves them beyond these images. In short, this way is so exalted and so wonderful in its effects that souls, who have spent only a short time in it, advance in a wonderful manner.

It is important that directors have a thorough knowledge of this subject. Without it, they would do great harm to these souls, for example, by making them work with the senses. Such activity is completely contrary to them, because God is drawing them to himself and wants them to follow him faithfully in this simple, mystical way. As soon as directors notice this attraction they should encourage them to follow it without interfering too much with their

interior life. However, they should warn them not to seek themselves in such prayer, and to be sincere, impressing on them the
necessity of being faithful to their vocation. Without giving any
external evidence of it, they ought to admire the perfection of this
way in them, and constantly encourage them not to abandon it.
They should inspire them always to go forward and adhere only
to God, who takes them captive that they might belong only to him.

Under the constant influence of this divine action, these souls
now live more in the spirit than in the senses. They are less depend-
ent on considerations, affections and aspirations which come from
their own activity. The director should study their external behavior,
and see that they are always composed in their actions. He should
also observe whether they generously follow the attraction of God
both interiorly and exteriorly. If, for example, he sees that they
are wanting in humility, simplicity, or prudence, then he must
promptly correct them.

This kind of elevation, so noble and sublime, is more of a
perpetual contemplation, than methodical prayer, because it greatly
surpasses the ordinary kind of meditation. And my purpose in
writing about it is to undeceive those who, for lack of experience,
think that such souls are deluded. They believe they are not really
praying, that they are doing nothing. But actually, this state is
far more exalted than the active states which preceded it. For
here, the activity comes more from God, and the soul responds
to it with an ardent and unfailing love. Hence, this state is very
profitable because it produces real perfection in the soul. And even
though the soul may seem to remain in the same state, that doesn't
matter, because the soul is more or less raised from there above
itself. And the less it knows about where it is, the better, for then
it is where it ought to be.

In short, this way is so unusual and so profitable that it is as
superior to the common way as gold is superior to other metals.
In this state the soul enjoys ineffable peace in great simplicity and
repose. Storms do not approach its serene heaven, except at a
great distance. And even though it may be very naked and abandoned like other souls, the storms still remain outside. They never
enter the deepest center where the soul lives in retirement. This

aspect of the mystical way, taken in its perfection, is a part of the supereminent life. But here it is still imperfect and quite remote from that life. Through it the soul is fixed in God by means of a contemplation and a nakedness of spirit and thought which become gradually more perfect, depending on the soul's fidelity. Now, the soul is more passive than active. For it is not like God to leave his work done imperfectly. If the soul is faithful in responding to him, He sometimes acts in it in a way that is known to the soul, but often in a way that is unknown to it. He does this in order to adorn and enrich it for the final stage of its perfection.

Quite often God uses this method in order to conceal men from themselves and to subdue them without harm. For this reason I am content with simply showing the excellence of this path to the best of my ability. I cannot praise the divine Majesty enough for exalting and glorifying the souls of his choice in this admirable way. Here the soul is lost and annihilated by the ineffable perception of the naked Divinity. All method should now be set aside, for the soul, by means of a vigorous and essential action, flies quickly and simply above all created things. In an incomprehensible manner it penetrates the naked Divinity, while in its deepest being it remains quite open and receptive. There God reveals himself to it nakedly, in a way that is suited to its capacity. Gradually its state becomes more perfect until the soul goes beyond this stage to one that is more hidden. In that state the soul is quite simply absorbed in the diverse and detailed intellectual manifestations which God grants it. The manner and savor of these mysteries of the Faith are ineffable, for it is an experimental knowledge so divine that, in comparison with it, every form of human perception is only crude earth and dark night.

These admirable insights and thoughts succeed each other in an increasingly lively and marvelous manner, so that the soul is completely penetrated by them, and remains dilated and transformed in the brilliance of this ineffable light. The Spirit of God moves it, as it were, by ravishing each of its faculties, or, it may be better to say, its whole being. For the time being, the inferior part of the soul is one with the superior part. The latter, under the influence of a loving and luminous attraction, recollects itself ever more profoundly in the abyss of its loving Object, in whom it is eternal as he is himself. This may make as much of an impression in the depth of such souls as the experience of eternity.

The reader must not think that I am saying the soul in this spiritual stage becomes perfect all at once. But once the soul is introduced into it, it will infallibly become perfect quite soon, if it places no hindrance to it. For the soul is now very humble. And even though it is above humiliations, still it cherishes them greatly when the occasion arises. Its pleasure is *to enter* and *to go forth: to enter* into the profound abyss of God where it is irritrievably lost in the sight of his infinite grandeur and beauty which it contemplates continually with the eye of its understanding; and *to go forth* from there to the ravishing sight of our Savior, the God-Man, whom it is inspired to follow by a lively imitation both interiorly and exteriorly.

Spiritual Direction and the Spiritual Director

Spiritual directors should keep their charges occupied for a long time with subjects that keep the senses occupied and are filled with considerations that can be transformed into various affections. However, they should not make them labor thus for too long a time, nor should they allow them to behave too sensibly in God's presence under pretext of gaining facility. That would throw them upon themselves. Such activity should only be carried out at certain intervals and then for a moderate length of time. It should be governed more by desire and the will, rather than by the senses. Directors should especially guard them from over-taxing their mind and reducing their activity to the level of the senses and the imagination. For they think that when they are engaged in such activity they are united to God. Directors who fail to foresee this or prevent it in its early stages do irreparable harm to their disciples. Hence, they should learn how to discipline the imagination gradually in order to spiritualize it. Then they will be able to apply themselves simply and rationally to the things of the spirit. But the more the director neglects this matter or delays in investigating it, the greater and more irreparable will be the harm done.

The practice of this point will require much time and patience both on the part of the director as well as of the directed, unless the work of both is assisted by God's secret and divine touches. These touches draw the soul in pursuit of the good thus discovered and enable it to do and to endure all that it learns on the field of loving combats.

Ordinarily, individuals may be classified as possessing either an intellectual nature or an affective nature. The former are inclined to make a thorough study of the various subjects to which they apply themselves. Now some souls in this group are by nature inclined to seek themselves when they experience a sensible desire for God, to speak to him and love him. In this they are only seeking their own interests, and not, as they think, God's interests. With the strength and facility that this inclination gives them, they are able to talk to God all day long. But it is without fruit, because they do not leave their senses and natural desires. Thus they satisfy only themselves, not God. They abound in affective conversations which are accompanied by certain natural delights. But when it is a question of really dying to themselves, as for example, when they are hurt by others either intentionally or unintentionally, they want no part of it. Besides, they are quite sensual in their desires, affections, words and works, and full of their own feelings. Everything they do is only a product of their self-love. And if they are not promptly and thoroughly enlightened on this matter, they will always live in themselves. The pity of it is that they constantly grow worse. In the beginning they may be gentle in conversation, but that is so only as long as no one offends them. However, when they are older they grow angry and are annoyed when given occasion for it. They are also continually inclined to impatience and resentment, because they are restless and undisciplined. Undoubtedly, many in this class remain in this state all their life.

Still some, when well directed, as it were, change their nature and habit in order to become intellectuals. They do this with the help of considerations which the director provides for this purpose. Thus they become rational-minded, and consider God as the sovereign good of all rational creatures, and finally, succeed in uniting themselves entirely to God by fervent and well ordered affections of a high degree.

But if the director is not on his guard, he will be easily deceived by the facile and subtle disposition (tendency) of these souls, considering them disposed for union with God and actual love of him, when in reality they are far from him, and lost in themselves. He must be very observant and cautious, in order to discover this trap right from the beginning of their direction. Once he has discovered that they are indeed drawn to themselves, without seeming to do so, he must withdraw them from self and lead them to rational and intellectual subjects. Such subjects have qualities that are quite contrary to their sensually affective nature, making them look for considerations outside of themselves and develop them to the point where they can be transformed into affections. In order to enter this path, the soul must either read a great deal about such matters, or receive much enlightenment from its director. The latter should always generously provide the kind of direction that will inspire and enkindle his disciples. But he should not expect them to return to intellectual considerations all at once, since that kind of activity is quite contrary to them. However, with skill and patience, he will gradually draw them from themselves. He should continue this line of direction until they are entirely detached from the senses, and begin to enjoy making considerations, and transforming them into acts of love.

There is another kind of nature which is very affective in the understanding, in that it wants to split hairs over every object and always wants to speculate. It can never have enough knowledge to satisfy its insatiable curiosity. But since such knowledge belongs rather to the director than to the directed, the understanding, so active and attached to its pasture, will only give it up with great difficulty. Such souls are completely withdrawn from feelings of love in the will. They do not know what a dilated and enkindled will is. Hence, through a false belief, they place their good in the knowledge they have and can have about God through more remote objects. Out of it they make a kind of ladder mounting from consideration to consideration as much as possible. But in doing so they make no allowance for the weakness that inevitably sets in.

They labor in vain and without fruit. They consider every kind of subject. And if they are learned, they dispute and build castles in the air. These are only products of an imagination that carries their mind away, where, no one knows. So they are as foolish, vain, fickle and quick to rouse their passions in conversation, as the most rude persons among ordinary people.

Beginners should receive quite simply the spiritual nourishment that their skilled and enlightened directors provide for them until the understanding is disciplined. When their interior is thus simplified, they will gradually enter the way of love and affection. However, directors will labor in vain, unless God blesses their efforts with his secret and divine touches. Therefore, they must make every effort to direct souls from extremes back to a middle course, i.e., from excessive use of the understanding to the exercise of affection. Thereafter, they should be able to use either faculty regularly, but they ought to keep a tight rein especially on the understanding, so that it does not take precedence over the will. For it is not as harmful for love and affection to exceed the understanding, as it is for the understanding to exceed love and affection. We have already explained the reasons for this elsewhere.

Directors must not set a definite time limit for the spiritual progress of their disciples, because, in these matters some are slow and others are quick and active for the course. But some, who have what we call an intellectual nature, are of a sufficiently good disposition, and have such an active and penetrating understanding that they manage to attain some degree of light and spiritual life. Once they arrive there, they cast themselves so deeply into God by their earnest application that they surpass all thoughts and images of creatures, no matter how holy they may be. Having thus attained to God, they are essentially and singularly dilated in him, that is, in his Essence. They remain there in happy repose as long as they have something with which to dilate themselves according to their knowledge and understanding. Nor do they cease this active dilation in God until their strength and knowledge are spent. Since they are inclined to this active form of understanding, they may rest content with it, as long as they have the strength and ability providing it does no harm. But once nature is satisfied and has spent its strength and capacity on this subject, it no longer wishes to return to it. And the reason is that it does not wish to make repeated inquiries for knowledge on matters with which it is already completely satisfied.

This practice is not bad. In fact it is good. The understanding is perfectly reformed by it even to the third and last degree required for perfection. Through it the soul is blest with perfect intelligence and becomes capable of casting itself into God in the twinkling of an eye. By means of profound dilations it plunges into him to such an extent that it goes beyond all that he is and over all that he possesses. But since the manner in which the understanding represents its object is simple and abstracted from the multiplicity of visible things, these souls are unwilling to come back again to visible things. They have no desire to use them in order to dilate[6] themselves in God. Now, through the strength of their simple glances and acts, they are in a moment drawn and plunged into him beyond all such notions. Already in this state, such souls unfortunately prefer rather to die of hunger than to leave their Object who absorbs and engulfs them in himself. Nor do they wish to come back again to specific objects, in order to use them as means to elevate and unite themselves to God. Such a practice is now insipid and wearisome, and seems contrary to justice and good sense.

Now let us suppose that they have spent themselves in effort, but not in desire. (In this their hunger is greater than ever and it subtly transports them to the good they possess and experience by the simple light of faith. Through it God manifests himself to them and draws them to himself by transcending the understanding.) This being the case, directors must carefully avoid spending themselves too much in furnishing their disciples with subjects for illumination and dilation. For, although they possess a spiritual abundance, unless they cease spending themselves so much, at least for a while, they will no longer have anything to give their disciples. Moreover, they would become dull and burdensome to them through their dilations which would now be forced and drawn by main strength from the senses. This point is one of the most subtle aspects of spiritual direction.

Let directors give their charges a short conference, in which they provide a few thoughts whose only purpose is to maintain them in their present state. Depending on his own abundance and the disposition of his disciples, he should sometimes develop these thoughts at greater length. But, in order to give them greater freedom for pleasant and suitable dilation without diverting them from their state—unless by subjects very closely related to their degree—I recommend giving them material for meditation from the last chapter of the *Garden of Contemplatives,* entitled, "The sanctifying action of the Spirit of God." Directors should arrange and digest what is most simple, direct and outstanding in it. With this external help, they should make their disciples dilate themselves simply and essentially in God as they consider his work in them and in all creatures.

They may experience some difficulty in this practice, but that will only be at the outset. However, they must make a beginning if they wish to maintain and preserve themselves in simple and profound introversion. For there is no other way of drawing these persons to motives and subjects that belong to the simple soul. By this means they will be able to recollect themselves quite simply in God. However, since their understanding is enlightened, simple, profoundly active and goes straight to its object, they cannot use subjects that enkindle the will and the understanding together. Such subjects are entirely opposed to the desire and action of the understanding. But the subjects of the above mentioned exercise lead to a vigorous love by way of knowledge. They refresh and sustain their spirit by arousing a strong desire for their sovereign Object. Thus, by a secret liquefaction, they will sink ever deeper into the divine abyss, where their whole pleasure will be to die continually in him.

Again, we must warn the director to be very careful with certain souls who are actively and madly inclined to this way. They are even more active than the souls discussed above. They give themselves neither relaxation nor repose as long as they feel they can act and desire. The result of such continued eagerness is that they finally surpass themselves, and enter into the obscurity and dark mist of the Divinity. There they find themselves without feelings and devoid of a savorous taste. They no longer have their accustomed strength to unite themselves to God. Confused, uncertain and ignorant of their state, their darkness often becomes a torment to them, unless they receive expert direction. Moreover, this state is the reason why they are so ignorant and incapable of judging things correctly. The worst part of it is, since they are imperfect, they will always remain shrouded in this dark obscurity, and ignorant of their ways, like the blind, who have no other certainty of the truth of their way except the intention to please God and to be obedient in all things. But in those matters of obedience which are not entirely prescribed, it would be difficult to describe how many indiscretions they commit in order to observe them. In short, their whole life is full of faults and mistakes, and attempts to escape from their spiritual state. But they will never find a way out. On the contrary, they will always sink deeper into it. Nor will they be any the more holy and better for it, unless they submit entirely to the guidance of a spiritual director.

Directors should carefully enlighten such persons. They should also detach them from their desires, and manage to interest them in matters that are outside of them and more external than their previous interests. Individuals in this condition are very difficult to instruct and direct. They are, as it were, in a continual hell, or at least in constant darkness. No one can convince them of anything, or tell them anything that might satisfy them.

1. I.e. dependence on the senses.
2. Cf. glossary.
3. Cf. glossary.
4. Cf. glossary.
5. Cf. glossary.
6. Cf. glossary.

CHAPTER II

PRAYER OF ASPIRATION[1]

Introduction

The teaching of John of St. Samson on aspiration must not be applied indiscriminately. The reader should take only what suits him. Let him remember that Brother John is talking only about acts of love and not about ejaculations, which include acts of the other virtues, besides love. Thus, acts of faith, hope, sorrow, etc. are ejaculations, but not aspirations as understood here. Now according to John, beginners in the spiritual life will only be able to practice aspirative prayer at certain intervals. First they must gain experience in meditation so as to be able to inflame the heart with acts of love. Then they should cultivate loving conversation with God. By this time they will be practicing affective prayer. It is then that they can seriously undertake to acquire aspiration as a *habit*. In its early state, aspiration is *profuse*, but gradually grows brief and concise in words, and finally, is reduced to one word. In its highest and most perfect form it is a simple inclination of the heart, consisting of an intense, burning glance or sigh of love, prolonged for some time. When aspiration becomes a habit, the soul is encouraged to practice the use of the four methods described below in this chapter; cf. p. 79 (*Translator*)

FIRST STAGE[2]

(*Definition*) Aspiration is not to be considered as merely a loving conversation. In itself this is a good practice, and from it springs aspiration. But aspiration as such is a loving, ardent transport of mind and heart which elevates the soul above itself and all created things, and seeks to be intimately united with God in the ardor of its loving desire. This desire, thus expressed, surpasses all sensible and comprehensible love. Under the impetus of the Spirit of God, and with its own cooperation, the soul arrives at divine union by a sudden transformation of the spirit in God. The spirit rises above all intelligible love in the abundant and ineffable sweetness of God himself, in whom it is lovingly submerged. Essentially this is aspiration both in its cause and in its effect.

Although aspirations are composed of only a few words, they lift the soul up entirely into God, and do not permit any sensible division between the two (i.e. *God and the soul*).

(*When to begin aspiration*)   The spiritual director must be careful not to encourage novices, who are making notable progress, either too soon or too late, in the practice of frequent aspiration. However, those who are properly disposed for it may be encouraged to begin the practice of a more remote kind of aspiration. Indeed, this exercise is practiced even in the active life,[3] although at intervals and very laboriously. When he sees that they are capable of producing prolonged affections easily, then he should instruct them in the theory of remote aspiration. But he should only give them as much knowledge as they need at the time, increasing it as they go from one degree to another, and from one state to another.

The director should carefully guard them from injuring themselves through too great a mental effort. It would be better not to admonish them too much. Then let him set up a clearly defined goal and a limited perfection beyond which, even his most promising disciples will not pass. For example, it would be beyond them to undertake the practice of pure and naked (*detached*) love through simple and prolonged aspiration.

Now, it is important not to begin this practice too soon, or sooner than I have indicated. However, in its general practice, it has a number of degrees. But he who earnestly gives himself up as a victim to divine love, will soon become so proficient that he will be able to discourse on this love in all its degrees and practices.

(*Caution*) The soul must avoid an excessive effort with head and heart, especially in the beginning. Otherwise, it may render itself unfit for this exalted and excellent practice which leads so perfectly and easily to a union above union, if one may so speak, of the lover with the Beloved. Therefore, the soul must be careful to practice it with discretion, and especially, avoid using it for its own pleasure. This would be contrary to the way of love and unworthy of it. For, although these elevations may be to the glory of God and the good of the creature, still his Majesty wishes the soul to preserve its energies sufficiently to perform the duties and tasks of life according to its vocation and state.

(*Who is not suited for it*) The way of aspiration is not suitable for those who are *only* sensibly and by nature affective,[4] even though they may seem to break their hearts by its practice. The reason is that they are excessively given to pleasing their own nature, which provides them with an abundance of sensible feelings under pretext of giving pleasure to God. They are at such cross purposes with God that they never have and perhaps never will have anything in them that will respond to his pure attractions. They live only according to the ways of nature, and very often are as burdened with all the sins of a disordered spirit as their opposites, the companions of true love, are adorned with all the virtues.

(*Who is suited for it*) On the other hand, those, who practice aspiration together with constant mortification, soon arrive at the summit of all blessings, and happily attain all its states and degrees without any harm. I believe this practice, taking it in a broad sense, is compatible with some small imperfections, but they must not be in any way voluntary. It is also compatible with mere human frailty and weakness. We must not be surprised at the loftiness of these ways, nor should we be afraid of not succeeding in them. Since there are various degrees and states in the way of aspiration, God will draw and elevate the soul according to its perseverance and fidelity to this exercise. He who gives less will receive less. He who gives much will receive much, and he who gives all and always, will receive all.

Those who make considerable progress in this divine science, (viz. *mental prayer*), are soon fitted for the practice of aspiration, especially if they are of an affectionate nature. But some will never be suited for it, or for occupation with God and in God by means of a simple and loving thought, which is a very excellent mystical practice.

It is quite certain, that, by ourselves, we cannot produce the savory and delicious feelings of love, unless his divine Majesty draws us to himself by his vivifying light which consumes all that it finds disposed for it. But it does so only to the degree of our fidelity in dying to self and in losing self in God.

Therefore, in the beginning of this practice it is absolutely necessary for us to die to ourselves, to humble and despise ourselves perfectly. For, by our sins, we have destroyed and annihilated the infinite grandeur of God as it existed in us. For this reason we should resolutely hate[5] ourselves, but with due discretion.

In order to combat the cursed enemy of sin as we ought, and the corrupt habits it has produced in us, we must constantly deny ourselves in all things. In doing so we should lean on God alone, trusting in him with a most filial and confident love. Then too, in all events, good or bad, we should seek God's good pleasure and his divine guidance.

Besides this, we ought to turn our mind and heart continually to the divine Presence. At the same time, in an attitude of profound humility which sees the nothingness of self and all things, we should live under God's all powerful hand, and consider ourselves beneath every human creature for love of him. As a means to accomplish this we should consider God's infinite greatness, and his external works. These works were not necessary for his glory nor to his best interests. First, there is the work of creation, by which we, as it were, became little gods, formed in the divine image. Then there is the work of Redemption. Seeing that we had miserably fallen from the state of his divine likeness, and become modeled in the image of the devil, the Lord, moved to compassion by his infinite goodness and love, at the appointed time, delivered us from eternal death, and from a painful and wretched slavery to our most cruel enemy, the devil.

The good God accomplished this for us at infinite cost to himself. He gave himself to us and took on the likeness of our humanity. Like us, he was subject to suffering. He was weak, poor, miserable and mortal. With the exception of ignorance and sin, he was surrounded by all our infirmities.

The infinite love of God, considered in itself as well as in the humanity which he assumed in order to make us God-like, ought to be a constant, loving occupation with us. But this cannot be done, except by the actual and persevering practice of constant death to self. Thus, our souls will be touched, elevated, illumined and sanctified by perfect love.

(*Method of practice*)   The practice of aspiration is laborious only in the beginning. When you acquire it as a habit, it becomes easy. But what costs nothing is considered of little value. Possessing the wonderful habit of love and a great facility in loving is ample reward for your labor.

All that is required in the beginning is that you practice aspiration faithfully and with good will, neither too sluggishly nor too much according to feeling. For a time you should make use of every possible subject that can inflame the will, until it has become a habit.

Take all visible things as a subject for aspiring to God. Gradually, aspiration will become more concise and will contain the truths of faith condensed in a more essential form in keeping with the desire of the will. As your soul receives the illuminations and the profound touches of God which contain various manifestations of his grandeur and beauty, together with an experimental knowledge of the nothingness of creatures, it becomes ever more interior, active and filled with yearning, but without labor on its part. It feels and sees itself lost, dissolved and transformed in this immense all-consuming fire. There, having risen above itself in its lofty elevation, it no longer lives any other life but the life of God, who animates and moves it by his Spirit.

In the beginning the soul uses a profuse kind of aspiration practiced at intervals. It should continue to act thus as long as possible. However, it should be prudent and avoid using too much effort and vehemence in forming these acts of love.

Therefore, those disposed for the practice of aspiration, ought to urge themselves moderately until their aspirations become more concise rather than profuse. It will then become sweet, sensible and enjoyable. Once they are accustomed to this laborious practice, they will find it easy to use any subject that is suitable for inflaming the will, but especially that of the divine favors. Thus, by means of ardent colloquies, they will become more expert in aspiration.

The way to produce these aspirations is to form certain exclamations, questions and requests for love, union, perfection, etc. The soul should continue to do this with a most ardent desire according to the requirements of the subject with which it is occupied. Mystical books are full of these loving darts. Let it be known, however, that a good aspiration is incompatible with voluntary imperfection. These passionate and flaming darts pierce the loving heart of God and compel him to pour himself out upon us. They enrapture the soul in him with an inexpressibly sweet and delightful ardor and impetuosity. Thus the soul learns by experience that love is sufficient for itself, and once acquired, it no longer needs methods or rules. Since it is ardent and luminous, it is also very fruitful and well instructed by the vivifying unction of the Holy Spirit, who pours it out abundantly together with himself.

In the beginning a person may not feel his heart moved or inflamed by the darts which he launches toward God. Nevertheless, this exercise is still good and holy. If one applies himself to it with fervor, he will finally feel himself drawn inwardly and stirred by divine love. This occupation does not put a strain upon the head, but it does affect the heart according to one's spiritual state. Of this exercise it may be said that one must eat his bread by the sweat of his brow, especially in the beginning. We must remember that love has neither peace nor repose, as long as it does not see its Object, or as long as it is not speaking to him, or does not feel itself to be perfectly one with him. It abhors what is external or what creates any difference with him, like death itself. In short, all its pleasure and its whole life are in him alone. Love often says to him, "My heart and my flesh have rejoiced in the living God"; they rejoice in him and always will rejoice in him.

Therefore, it is better to open one's heart in actual fact by an actual and persevering love, rather than to do so by aspirations selected and memorized from books. This is the easier way to acquire real love. Nevertheless, rather than remain idle and sterile, one may turn to those aspirations which are to be found in mystical books, using them as if one had composed them for himself.

(*In prayer*) The actual feeling and consciousness of the divine Presence ought to keep the soul, together with all its faculties, constantly attached to God. This can be done by cultivating a strong and ardent desire which will enable it to possess him with a perpetual and simple tranquility of heart. But to do this well, the soul must converse with him interiorly by loving and intimate conversations. Picture to yourself the familiar and intimate conversation of two close friends: their gestures, their actions, their demeanor, their mutual and sincere affection for each other and their conversation. Act in the same way with his divine Majesty: humbly, sweetly, familiarly and freely, (always however, with great respect). In due time, you will become his kingdom and his whole delight, and your soul, as spouse of such a King, will indeed be a queen forever, by a perfect union with him.

But, in order to converse with God in this manner, you might use such themes as his grandeur, or better yet, his infinite love and goodness. Out of love for us and for our own good he came to us (wretched and miserable as we are) in a most wonderful way. He gave himself to us, and united us to himself, because of what he is and what he does in us. When we have acquired the ability to carry on a loving conversation, ... we can say that we repose in our final Object. The contemplation, knowledge and feeling of this divine Object ought to have such influence over us that, henceforth, we should forget to think of earthly things, and even of ourselves.... Then we shall be like the soul that devotes its whole life entirely to this practice.

In the beginning, and whenever rebellious feelings force themselves upon our attention, it is good to do a little violence to ourselves, until we have learned to rise above the senses and sense
images. The soul should continue to act in this way (i.e., *by aspiration*), until it is conscious of success, and is at once able to unite
itself to God. But if these animal[6] feelings are too insistent and
too strong to be overcome at one time, or even for some time,
then we should postpone this violent combat until we have somewhat
recovered our strength. Then we should return to the combat with
the same vigor as before. Nor should we cease to behave thus in
the second attempt, or even the third attempt, until we have gained
the victory. What great satisfaction! What incomprehensible delights for the Spouse and for the bride who is encouraged in this
combat by his divine Presence. Sometimes, the Spouse seems to be
quite far from her, but she always enjoys the satisfaction of her
victory, and the pleasure of his hidden Presence. He inspires her
in this combat by a secret satisfaction and by a strength that
remains hidden in her and is intended only for her.

Aspiration, practiced as a familiar, respectful, and loving conversation with God, is such an excellent method, that, by means
of it, one soon arrives at the summit of all perfection, and falls
in love with Love. But the practice of aspiration as a continual
exercise must come after one has become proficient in meditation,
and has attained a certain ease in affective prayer. I say easy and
affective to show that here one must not fill the understanding
with curiosity. Once the understanding has examined and sufficiently understood the divine works, it ought to pass them on to
the will, in order to be inflamed and nourished by them. Just as
a hunting dog, when he has taken the prey, is not allowed to
keep it, so the understanding should not be allowed to enjoy the
light and truth that has been discovered more than is necessary.
We should not allow the understanding to brouse over it without
restraint. But when it has sufficiently penetrated the truth, then
the will should receive it as its own supernatural nourishment,
in order to be aroused and inflamed by it as much as possible.
Here it is the will that does all in this exercise. But for a long
time, consideration should precede aspiration, because affection needs

the preceding movement of the understanding and its enlightened presentation. Then, under the influence of the love of God, it at once embraces this knowledge, arousing and enkindling itself by it.

In the beginning the understanding must draw the will after it and inflame it by using motives based on love. Now, if the soul delights in contemplating Love both in Itself as well as in Its effects, and perseveres in this loving activity, God, in His goodness and mercy, will infallibly assist it. For He never fails to anticipate, help and strengthen the soul that humbly desires to attain this infinite Love.

First, practice aspiration at long intervals by means of loving conversations. You should enkindle in yourself the desire to love Love in himself, above all the manifestations of his love in nature, grace and glory. Just as men excite admiration in each other over the many evidences of a king's goodness and love, so also, and for even greater reason, should you excite in yourself a constant wonder and rapture over the marvels of God's infinite love. He appeared among us poor and miserable creatures, and manifested himself in many supernatural ways to his own infinite glory and for our good. Therefore, since "it is in him that we live and move and are," we must also flow back into him by a very active and an unfailing love. We must do this not only to know him in an eminent degree, but also to love him constantly and most ardently. For this reason we should rejoice in him with the whole of our being, as we look forward to the fullness of eternal bliss.

An effective means to begin aspiration is to meditate on divine love. But loving converse is even more effective and more conformed to this practice. From it, as from a very fruitful and fertile field, aspiration takes its beginning.

(*During work*) God expects us to leave ourselves for the performance of the external works which are a part of our state of life, and are commanded by our superiors. If it is manual work, it should only apply the body to it, while the mind rests sweetly in the loving bosom of God. At the same time, we should carefully avoid working with too much haste.

When some important work comes up, which demands all your

attention in order to be planned and done well, give all your attention to it for a certain determined time. After that, do not think of it any more. If the task is very difficult, when you have determined the means to accomplish it, file it away in your memory, so that you may no longer be importuned by images of it either before or after your prayers. This method is very good for quieting the mind which must be occupied with business affairs. But if, after this, you are still harassed by these images, you must energetically reject them as things that are irrelevant and distracting. You will do this with greater facility, if you write down what you plan to do.

When you study or read, do so, according to your degree of love, in all purity and holiness. Often raise your eyes from the book and direct a loving glance toward God in a simple aspiration like this. "I read and study, O my Love and my life, not so much to acquire knowledge and learning, as to love you, and to become sufficiently learned and capable to perform the duties of my office."

When you have done all that is necessary to accomplish a task well, leave the care of circumstances that may eventuate entirely to God, without troubling yourself any further over the matter. Be as content with whatever God arranges in the affair, as you would be if you knew his most holy will for certain.

"O Goodness! O immense Love! You wished to create creatures as manifestations of your divine and eternal thoughts, that they might know you, love you and always live in harmony with your surpassing love. You created them to know and love you alone above all other things, so that they might thus always remain adorned with your divine likeness, the source of their beauty and supernatural fulfillment.

"What is the purpose of all this, O Lover of angels and men? How great a distance there is between being and nothing, from which everything was created with such great and eminent perfection! If the angel has reason to marvel at the vast infinity of your Majesty, at its love and beauty, how much more reason have we to marvel at it, who are nothing in comparison to the angelic nature!

"So then, they and we are the admirable results of your ecstatic love, love which enraptures the blessed angels and holy men. It is there that you produce results which are powerful enough to annihilate men who do not correspond to your action in them. They receive much, and spoil everything that you give them by putting it and themselves to bad use. Yet, my Beloved, how content and peaceful they are in their own natural comfort, without so much as even a thought of you, who are their existence and all their good.

"But I, Lord, who am I? From whence have you drawn me through creation and redemption, if not from the mire and from all corruption, from a most wretched state in which I was blind to the work of love. You did this O Lord, in order to make me sit among the princes of your elect, your chosen people.

"O Love, O Goodness, O boundless Mercy! O infinite Majesty, who fills everything and sanctifies every man who comes into the world and does not love it! Who can measure what you have accomplished even in me, and what you have made of me? No one, Lord. No one would know how to do it. For I feel myself exceedingly obligated to your infinite Majesty both for what it is in itself, as well as for all the benefits I have received from it in body and soul according to nature and grace.

"If I consider only the natural blessings, how can I forget the many favors I have received that merit admiration! And as for the supernatural favors I have received, even beyond those of baptism and of vocation, where shall I begin, seeing that I have so little merit and deserve so little, unless it be through your special grace and love?

"No, my Love and my Life, I am speechless with admiration, for I own nothing that belongs to me. And if I have anything, namely myself, I am so poor and so weak, that I continually fall into the abyss of all corruption.

"But, since you, my Love, have given me dominion over myself through my free will, therefore, as far as I am able, I freely give myself back to you as a pure and an eternal holocaust. O Truth, so new and so eternal, I am exceedingly sorry to have known and loved you so late!

"How often have creatures, by their easy lives, asked me, Where is your God? And I did not give the right answer. For you are in me as in your own kingdom. But I did not always know this with the kind of knowledge and love that freely urged me to look for you, to feel you, to love you and to possess you in myself. That is why I am so sorry, my Beloved.

"What greater misery can be imagined than to live in and for oneself, without ever living according to the maturing influence of God's love in oneself. O my Life, did you not say that I ought to be as perfect and holy as you are? Yet I was deaf to your words and did not answer your call.

"But now, my Love, regretting this misfortune, I wish to set to work in real earnest without let-up or self-indulgence. Now I wish to return to you with my whole heart and my whole mind, and to love you forever, no matter what the cost.

"Alas! My Love! My heart has been continually disturbed by the past like the sea lashed by a furious storm. I have lived irresolutely, and without peace of heart, and did not know the cause of my misery.

"The heart that does not love you, my Beloved, is nothing but a den of thieves, where each thief tries to draw the heart to himself, in order to have his share of it. Such a man is so miserably outraged by his voluntary guests, that his wretched captivity is beyond description. Each of his guests contributes to his misery for fear of the prize escaping him. O inconceivable misery of men, compounded a thousand times over! Such men are all the more miserable in proportion to the pleasure they take in their wretched servitude, for they are only subjecting themselves to a host of wretched masters!"

From this example you can see love's great capacity. As it grows, it becomes more concentrated through ardent and burning aspirations. Every thing is food for love. It has no plan or schedule. At all times it sends forth the burning flames of its heart simply and abundantly. It ignores all discretion, means and measure, because its Well-Beloved ravishes it by his sweet attraction and enchanting beauty. There it wishes to be irretrivably lost, desiring only to sink ever more deeply into it.

SECOND STAGE

(*Definition and degrees—Speaking of pure love*)   The manner of practicing this ardent and lively love is short and easy. Its subject is constant and loving aspiration. But to be perfect, aspiration must be practiced so eagerly and continually that it becomes as easy as breathing. It has a number of degrees, all of which can be reduced to four.[7] They are like four hammers with which the soul knocks strongly at God's door, in order to enter into him with its whole being. Now the *first degree* or method consists in offering oneself and all created things to God. As far as possible this should be done in an abstract manner (i.e., *spiritually, or detached from sense feelings*). For how long a time it should continue this depends on the soul's fidelity. The *second degree* consists in making requests of the divine Spouse, asking him for his gifts both in him and for his own sake. The *third degree* consists in being resigned and completely conformed to him. This conformity is very lofty and perfect, and is characterized by great love. Moreover, the soul also desires it for all creatures who are capable of such an elevated love. The *fourth degree* is that of unitive love which unites the soul to God. Here the soul yearns for him and pursues him with acts of love until he opens his loving and superessential bosom to it. Here it feasts upon his immense beauty in great abundance and intoxication, eating and drinking at the table of the Blessed. But since this does not last very long, the soul soon returns to itself to feed upon its former spiritual fare. From this it derives renewed strength, until God again receives it into his bosom with the same effect. This degree is very exalted and contains the preceeding degrees in their most perfect form. However, the first three degrees may also be practiced with a profound and perfect union outside of the last one. This depends on the soul's progress in aspiration. But in the last degree, the soul's only occupation, by which it seeks its Well-Beloved, is that of union itself.

These four degrees are the principal means by which the soul actively expresses its love for the Spouse. By the zealous practice of them, it will attain an even greater perfection in God. It will then go from one abyss of profound delight to another, until it reaches the ultimate abyss—infinite in depth—where the soul will be wholly lost in God and swallowed up with exceeding joy in its eternal Origin.

Those who are capable of loving and have made some progress in the spiritual life should resolve to love God constantly and fervently during prayer and outside of it by the practice of simple aspirations. Although they are composed of only a few words, they lift the soul up entirely into God, and do not permit any sensible division between the two (i.e., *God and the soul*). Once it has experienced these effects in the way advanced souls do, it will be quite convinced that aspiration is an effective means to acquire the highest perfection. In its practice let it use only the best motive, namely, pure love. Such love does not need reasons to be convinced into loving its divine Object.

(*Benefits and effects*)   The soul that has faithfully practiced these exercises is bound to see and feel the effect of this truth (i.e., *union with God through aspiration*) by experience. Indeed, if it is faithful to this practice it will often feel itself drawn and completely transported out of itself by sublime, anagogical[8] aspirations. In this state it will experience the overwhelming pleasure of being dissolved and liquified. There it will enjoy sweet and abundant delights in the *superessential*[9] bosom of the Spouse, its Paradise. Still, this is not quite the depth, nor the height of the elevations which can be attained by this practice.

(*After aspiration has become a habit*), the soul will find it necessary to take up the method of the four kinds of aspiration. This method we defined and explained elsewhere, indicating that it should become the foundation of aspiration. For, if the soul practices it faithfully, it can, without too much human assistance, attain the summit and enjoyment of the superessential[10] life, viz., the continual enjoyment and contemplation of God, beyond action and above created things, and the experience of his own enjoyment in supreme action and passion.

Here I seem to have prescribed certain kinds of aspiration and

subjects for it. This, however, does not apply to those who have
become well-versed in this holy practice, as in the instance mentioned above, of the soul that is eminently enlightened. In this
stage the soul should allow itself to be carried away by the impulses
and desires of its impetuous love, and on whatever subject it pleases.
But the subject will never be anything else than the divine Object,
which it desires so much. For it seeks to make its Divine Spouse
see how greatly it is enamoured of him and moved by his singular
love. In this eminent degree the spouse is completely lost and absorbed in its Beloved. Here it becomes one with him in his infinite
and most simple love.

This particular way of aspiration which we have explained as
being mystical, is rather broad. Its final and most lofty effect is
that the inferior, sense powers are greatly dilated[11] and elevated
to a high degree. At this time they undergo the marvellous effects
of *divine inebriation*. The mystics express it under the terms *'wine'*
and *'drunkenness,'* because the profuse effects of it are similar to
those produced by wine and natural inebriation.

It would be impossible to say how much prudence, understanding
and experimental knowledge loving souls receive in the practice
of aspiration. All this is received by means of very simple savors
and delights. In such souls the Holy Spirit pours out his love.
It would be equally impossible to describe the loving experiences
these souls will have, for example, the clear knowledge of their
sins, and after that, of their more hidden imperfections; also, an
insight into the goodness and perfection which divine Love demands
of them. All this they will certainly see and know with astonishment and confusion, together with a loving compunction and joy
experienced in diverse ways. It will continually strengthen them
in this excellent practice, and humble them profoundly in the divine
abysses. They will be so humbled that they will not know what
response to make to the infinite Love which absorbs and totally
engulfs them in the infinite immensity of a most ardent and consuming fire.

When you are penetrated by the sweetness of love and are drawn
into Love itself, you will see what an obstacle images are, and
how created things hinder the soul's entrance into God. But the

fervent practice of aspiration will free you from this obstacle, and keep you naked, simple, peaceful, free and very recollected. You will be like a well-polished mirror, that clearly reflects the excellence and beauty of God within, and the Sacred Humanity of your beloved Savior and Spouse without. Thus you will be both interiorly and exteriorly calm, like the faithful lover who always lives in the presence of God, his Well-Beloved.

He who practices aspirative love has this characteristic, namely, he changes and reduces all things to his outlook, and believes that all have his own disposition. When this is not the case, he leaves matters as they are, without otherwise burdening himself with them, and pursues his own way, keeping a constant and simple gaze fixed on his Object. His only desire on every occasion is to please and satisfy God alone with an ardent and singular love.

The soul's only rule and guiding motive is the infinite will of God, and consequently, God himself. Thus it never leaves its Object in any way whatever, and never entertains thoughts unworthy of it, not even on occasions of the greatest sufferings and deaths. It considers such sentiments and reflections unworthy of a generous soul, who desires to rise above all things. In fact such a soul does rise above them, far above them, through the power of its active or passive love. If at times it seems to entertain unworthy thoughts, that is only for a moment. At once its love and patience plunge it into the infinite abyss of Love.

(*Caution*)   Be on your guard against doing violence to your natural powers or impairing them by practicing aspiration too much with the senses. To act thus would be to place a wall between the soul and the Spouse, and consequently, would render it unfit for quick and perfect union. Besides, the soul would become a victim of serious disorders. These elevations ought to be produced more within the soul rather than in the senses. For to wish to enclose God within the confines of animal (sense) feeling is greatly to deceive oneself. The supreme happiness of the spouse is not found there, but in a vigorous action that is detached from the senses, and, by its power, unites spirit and sense to its supreme and divine Object.

Effort that is too violent and too sustained harms head and

heart. To form very ardent aspirations constantly, when under the influence of abundant consolations, would gradually destroy our nature. Soon, through weakness of mind and body, we would no longer be fit for what concerns the soul, nor, perhaps, fit even for the labors of the body. Therefore, when we feel profoundly drawn in all our powers, so that the heart is, as it were, boiling in the intense ardor of this divine fire, then we should simply endure the divine action. We should withdraw somewhat from its vehement action by performing some external work, rather than produce acts which, at this time, are more harmful than useful, and are accompanied by self-seeking. Indeed, what need is there for stirring up our affections in what is already quite affective due to the loving attraction of God. On these occasions he carries the soul off into himself with great power.

Moreover, once the soul is ardently inflamed with love, it knows and observes neither method nor limit. Therefore, let it always be understood that discretion is to be observed in order to avoid interior and exterior disorders in one's nature. When the soul is not able to observe discretion, or when love does not permit it to do so because of its disposition, these disorders can affect its reason.

You must not over-tax your brain, nor do violence or harm to your faculties by aspiration. Proceed gently and with a moderate activity, that is as reasonable as it is sensible. You need not weary yourself if you can help it. Rest for a time, without making acts, except with the spirit, in order to refresh your faculties which have been overstrained. Meanwhile, continue to contemplate your infinite Object with great wonder by means of a simple gaze, and in profound silence. Continue thus, until you feel yourself lapsing from this state, and until nature recovers itself. Then, once more, begin making humble, devout and loving aspirations gently and at frequent intervals. Adopt this method as a normal practice.

There are those of a sensual nature who are great lovers of themselves. Their love and affection come only from a natural softness. Hence, the practice of aspiration is not suitable for them. But it is suitable for those who have acquired a very pure and spiritual love through a reasoned love, and through the operations of God in them. Consequently, we are not writing this for infants, nor for the soft and weak, but for souls who are generous, very hardy and strong, the true spouses of our Savior. I say very strong throughout the whole course of his infinite love (i.e., *to meet all the demands of divine love*), so that he may renew and exalt his divine likeness in them with ever greater perfection. But he who undertakes this practice on his own without guidance, will only find rocks, crags and precipices in it.

(*Method of practice*) Actual love is the cause of love and increases it to the highest possible degree. But those who have not yet attained perfect love must work strictly on the virtues and that out of love for God. They should persevere until they have acquired them as habits and have such a strong desire for them that they can practice the virtues on every occasion. Therefore, I advise souls in this state (i.e., *of pure love*) to be as active as possible, and eagerly to invent affectionate ways of conversing and uniting themselves with God. Such behavior makes the soul extremely expert in forming simple and familiar aspirations. At the same time, it enables the soul always to avoid the slightest differences with God in its desires, words and actions.

For advanced souls there is no definite method of aspiration. Such a method applies only to beginners. The mystics did not intend to teach a particular system. If they did so, it was to make the practice of aspiration easier. All souls may adapt it to suit their degree of active love, without worrying about how many acts to make, or in what way to make them. However, their interior activity ought to be lively, ardent and detached from the senses. Moreover, they may use any subject whatever, as long as it is concerned with union through love.

The way of aspiration demands the uniform practice of all the virtues. For this reason, the mystics say that, in this practice, the virtues are the body, and a very ardent and strong unitive love is the soul of it. In proportion as it becomes divine, this love becomes subdued in order to be able to bear all the operations of the divine fire in it. Even though the soul is completely rent by the wound of love within itself, it encounters no injury, weakness or hindrance from its physical nature.

The way to attain love is to love. A less excellent love leads to a greater love, and a greater love in turn leads to the highest love, as well as to the most excellent and ultimate fruits of active love. Each of these degrees has its own theory and practice. All of them (especially the last degrees) possess a simple, exalted, and singular contemplation of the divine Object, which constantly exerts a powerful influence on the soul and ravishes it with delight.

The practice of aspiration is laborious in the beginning, but easy and pleasant as the soul advances. In the end the soul literally flies by the exalted perfection of its aspirations. Little by little they are reduced to a few according as the soul enters heart and soul into God, and as the transformation of the subject into the Object is accomplished by means of frequent and subtle acts of love. Hence, as the soul advances and perfects itself in the loss of its being in the infinite unity of God, formulas and even the word *'love'* are done away with. For then the subject is happily transformed in the love of God, with whom it discourses more by way of supereminence[12] rather than by the expression of its great love. Still it does so, but under very simple forms.

Although love may be present in all the subjects of aspirative prayer, it only becomes perfect through the action of love itself. This alone becomes the final means ordained to attain its end most perfectly, viz. the total loss of the soul in God.

(*During prayer*)   When the soul has made notable progress in forming lively and frequent aspirations it will need only a simple, intense glance to plunge it into God as it contemplates his beauty without the use of forms or images. During this intuitive and joyful action, the soul is completely lost and dissolved in the divine Unity. While this lasts (actually a short time), the soul is completely renewed, and receives new strength in order to continue its interior action.

However, this intuitive and simple introversion comes to an end once the soul finds itself occupied with the senses and with sense objects. Then it should revert to its own brisk and dilated action, depending on the degree of aspiration it has attained. In spite of the distance between these two extremes, the soul feels it has great strength to act, and does so with little effort. In this way it succeeds in attaining once more the state of simple introversion. Happy, infinitely happy is the soul that perseveres in this exercise of love! For it is given to taste fully the exquisite delights of the loving assaults and communications of its Well-Beloved.

When you are recollected, address your Spouse with this loving aspiration: "Thou and I, my Love, Thou and I, and no one else besides! Thou art that Goodness and Essence which fills every essence and every being. It is Thou, who dost work in every being, who preserves and perfects it. Having no bounds or limits, Thou art beyond all understanding. For me, nonentity that I am, Thou art the end and the infinity of being. In Thee the love of the divine Being and the love of the created being are united as one." You might also use this aspiration: "O my· Love and my Spouse, I will entertain you. I will feast you with the wine of my pomegranates, a secret only for us!"

Those who have a sufficient knowledge of God and have reached the stage of simplified prayer, ought to urge themselves moderately to form essential[13] aspirations. The subject of these aspirations might be the benefits of God in general, or one of them in particular, or Divine Love and its effects. For want of this they remain idle, not knowing what to do, because of their nakedness (*detachment*) and inability to act. But this is not so much an inability to act as it is a failure of the will to apply itself to subjects that are suitable for inflaming it. For the will ought to be actively at work in some manner in order to be suitably occupied with God.

When the soul has been deeply touched, it is by love alone that it desires to be intimately joined to God. This is why we advocate reducing ardent aspiration to a few words, even to the mere word '*love*.' This love sends forth ardent and fiery flames with all its strength. As a result, a blazing divine fire is enkindled in the soul. It is in this way that God stirs up the soul and draws it strongly inwards.

God's purpose in this is to lose the soul, to dissolve and melt it in the immense furnace of his love, so that henceforth, it may there live a very calm and delightful life. So the soul does not rest until it has acquired this lofty, divine love, and until it has received the grace that efficaciously produces it. God responds by pouring it into the soul with great power, so that it completely consumes his devoted lover. On its part, the beloved soul gives itself most generously to this love which draws and ravishes it into God. Thus the soul is completely united and transformed into him.

There the soul enjoys the ineffable embraces and secrets, the grandeur and goodness of this God of love. After generous perseverance in responding to his graces, God draws the soul into the divine Abyss. In truth, it is submerged and baptized in the river of the most delicious fire of the Holy Spirit. Here it is filled with secret and delightful thoughts about all that pertains to his great glory [or, its eternal glory], as also to the beauty, splendor and immensity of God. So the habit of aspiration, in the course of time, becomes very strong, exalted and spiritual, and the soul uses it quite naturally to elevate itself and to be dissolved in the fire of love.

This way is quite fittingly called the mystical way, because it is hidden from those who tarry long in the senses. Such souls raise themselves up to God through the knowledge of sensible things, and through the activity of their understanding. Still, this in itself would be quite an achievement if they really sought to know him as much as possible in this common way without seeking themselves, and if they also added ardent affections without loitering in a subtle speculation which they call contemplation. While giving them much satisfaction, this speculation actually draws them away from God to some truth. Most often it draws them into themselves, and not into God. Besides, they are not at all elevated, except in their own nature, which, while giving them certain very pleasant savors, persuades them to believe that they are contemplatives, and that they have access to God. In reality, they are as far from him as they are full of themselves. In short, although they are inquisitive contemplators of all the virtues, these men are unmortified animals, who adore themselves and the subtle idols they have invented.

The soul must practice this first way of contemplation[14] for at least one good year with every possible effort, until it feels greatly illumined and inflamed by love. After that it will enter more easily and advantageously into the way which is secret and mystical.

This way is a wisdom that fills the soul with infinite splendor and delights, a divine science that carnal men cannot comprehend, because it is divinely infused through gratuitous love. The animal man considers it a madness, since an early effect of this way is to overwhelm the senses and the powers of the soul. It becomes simple and one in the fire of love which consumes its whole being. Here it is held in a profound, luminous and delightful embrace beyond all expression. Simple within, it now becomes entirely spirit in the Divine Spirit, in whom it is more acted upon than acting. In this state the soul experiences more of enjoyment than it does labor, although one or the other may be present. It is labor when the soul must perform external works. Moreover, when it is not strongly drawn by God, it labors with its whole being in forming the most delicate acts of love. But when the soul is ardently transported into the immense sea of the most simple Divinity, the experience is so delightful that it is like paradise on earth. Then God produces various transports in the soul as well as manifold states of purity, splendor and perfection not to mention various simple delights and other effects. For such a soul it is simply beyond words.

When the soul is accustomed to aspiration, it becomes as easy as breathing. Then it can turn to the simple and delightful consideration of the divine perfections, which is an excellent practice. After this comes the loss of self. But the purely mystical way, which is the very flow of wisdom reduces everything to itself, that is to say, to God, whom it sees and tastes with constant delight.

If it is not very spiritual, the soul should first begin this practice with profuse aspiration. But if it is more advanced and has an evident facility, it can make shorter and more concise aspirations to stir the heart. These darts will help to penetrate and open the heart, so that it may be touched and dilated by God, and may repose in him at will in time of ardent and sensible attraction. But it must not spend the time in considering itself, rather should it consider the work of God who draws it to this divine repose. In proportion as it advances in perfect love, the soul will quickly learn all that it ought to know and do. It will then become learned in the science of divine love.

When the soul is accustomed to be recollected and lost in God, the entire lower man becomes subject to the spirit. All actions of the senses therefore, also belong to the spirit. So simple and unifying is this state that it can enrapture the soul to the point where it no longer feels any opposition between either of these parts (i.e., *the senses and the spirit*).

The exclamations of such a soul, if it can still form any when it is entirely lost in the depths of its spirit, might be the following, "O Love! O Majesty! O Beauty! O Essence of all essence! O infinite Love! Infinite Mercy! O my All! O my dear Spouse! O my Life! O consuming Fire! O infinite Goodness!" etc. When you feel full of wonder over the beauty and marvels of God, you might use these burning exclamations for aspirations. Between exclamations there ought to be an interval pause. One of them might be repeated several times. In due time there will be loving ecstasies, which will come from overflowings of love, grief and wonder. All of this is caused by anagogical love and a total loss of the creature in the immensity of God, into which the soul has now fallen as into a fathomless abyss never to leave it.

But if the inward glance of the soul is very ardent and penetrating, it will not be necessary to form long drawn out acts which are repugnant to its heart's desire, for it now has something much better. However, the soul must be very observant, in order to see if it can form extended and dilated acts, and when it can, to do so. For without this attention and practice, it would be more idle than active.

If the soul feels a great repugnance to these acts, it is a clear sign that there is no need for them then, since the strength of its gaze holds it attentive and recollected in the contemplation of its Object, God. But if this gaze is not a habit of long standing, it will only last a short time and will only raise the soul to the contemplation of its Object for as long as it lasts. In this case however, after being quite absorbed in loving colloquies, the soul ought to stir itself up inwardly by a lively and steady vigilance over self, recollecting all its powers in unity and maintaining a steadfast gaze upon the Object that draws it. When its attention is drawn away from this to itself, it ought to begin once more to make its own acts. By acting thus it will avoid that false spiritual idleness which is much to be feared here. For he who takes appearances for the truth is very idle indeed. Some seem to think that, because they have sometimes felt a certain sweet and strong attraction which has raised them above sensible things to the contemplation and enjoyment of God, they are always in that state. This however, lasts only a certain time. When this happens, they have only to maintain the gaze by which they are drawn while it lasts. Then they might use ardent expressions like the ones I have indicated elsewhere, or make secret and unspoken loving laments in the depths of the soul. This is very easy for the soul that has become spiritual, because it has received it with love and light. However, when the soul becomes fully conscious of itself, it must form its own acts with a wide-open heart.

Entrance into the way of aspiration is easy for affectionate natures, but difficult for those who have not such a nature. The former are transported with love for God without too much knowledge, because the Divine Object, which enraptures them so strongly, quickly captivates their will together with the understanding. In many, this love is so strong that only the will enters the loving bosom of God. There it savors him with ineffable delight beyond all understanding, while the intellect remains at the door, as it were, suspended in wonder.

All this is due to the stream of burning love which pours into God's lovers. It enraptures and overwhelms them with its torrents. As far as it is possible in this life, they become like God in his spirit and divinity. Here nothing is either past or future, or even eternal. All is present in this delicious ocean. When the soul returns from this state, it sees that it is less than a small dot or an atom. Then it soars anew into God, into a vast infinite expanse where it desires to be swallowed up, so that it may live his life rather than its own.

Thus, this love becomes its own fruit. It is so supernatural and divine that it is both means and end at the same time. Means, insofar as the creature lovingly contributes to it; and end, insofar as it reposes there in love, joy and ineffable delight, gazing upon the ravishing beauty of God, who holds it, as it were, asleep in his loving bosom.

Those who are at liberty to act ardently and vigorously, while in a high degree of love, ought to do so both in contemplation as well as in action. They should let themselves be transported and enraptured over any subjects or thoughts which God may inspire in them. Moreover, let them revere all his diverse operations in their soul without reflecting on them any more than is necessary. They need only go their way and be equally content in poverty and abundance, in light and darkness, in life and death, always following the loving attraction which they experience.

Now these souls will be dilated and bound by a more essential love in proportion as they advance in this way of love. But this ought to be done by very simple and essential means. With time and practice the faculties will be deprived of their power to act. Then the soul will find it necessary to form aspirations consisting of only a few words by means of a simple, elevated and enlightened love, and at frequent intervals. It should follow the loving attraction which draws and excites it to turn to its Well-Beloved and be dissolved in him.

Souls, accustomed to use the will in mental prayer, ought to finish it with ardent, heartfelt affections. Indeed, if they could always pray thus, it would be excellent prayer. For to tell the truth, the union of the soul with God is only accomplished by the active use of the will inflamed with love for its divine Object. From this we may readily conclude that the practice of aspiration belongs to the will. When it is wanting, then the actual reformation of the soul and its transformation in God are also wanting. Therefore, to achieve this it must resolve to exercise itself in profound, ardent laments and burning sighs. These should be constant and as perfect as possible.

If the soul does this faithfully, it will find, with time, that it has attained a high degree of perfection and union with God. It will have easy access to the more simple and exalted degrees of aspiration which carry the soul to the highest degree of transforming love, from God into God himself. It is in this continual and divine exercise that the paradise of God in the soul and of the soul in God consists. For what purpose ought it to use every moment of life if not to live wholly in God by the power of his love.

In the practice of this spiritual exercise the soul may consider the multitude of its sins in general, but never in particular. For this exercise is more suitable and agreeable to *proficients* than to beginners. Sometimes, out of admiration, when it feels the grandeur, goodness and sweetness of God flowing into its sense faculties, the soul may once more present to God the whole of its past life in general. This experience, and the effects of it, are so great and so moving that the soul does not know what to do. So great is its joy and admiration over the goodness which it sees, tastes and possesses. It exceeds created capacity. Even when this period of super-abundance is past, the after effects still stir up desire and admiration in the soul, and strongly urge it to serve God and please him perfectly. Those who practice this exercise must be exteriorly well composed, hold a middle course in everything and avoid extremes. For this reason, these souls ought to have planted crosses[15] long before this at the approaches of their interior and exterior senses.

(*During trials*) When you are harassed by creatures, or even by your superiors beyond all right and reason, stir up your love for God, not by long aspirations, but by simple, fervent sighs, acts and looks that are frequently repeated and launched toward him with all your heart. Do the same when you are very sick. If you are enduring great pain, especially in the head, the best thing to do is to turn and unite yourself to your Spouse by the simplest sighs, acts and looks. It will not matter if they are not so frequent. For the faithful lover, however, it will be as impossible to refrain from these aspirations as it is for the stone, thrown up into the air, not to fall back to its center of gravity.

Learn to make quick flights to God with an ardent and continual love, and thus rise completely above self and all created things. When you are able to do this, sorrow will be as foreign to you as if it did not exist. The reason is, if you persevere in inward recollection, you will always be quite joyful and content in every eventuality with all the joy, glory and happiness of God, who will be your all in all. But that will only come to pass when you have completely disappeared and are lost in him. But before you arrive there, you must first rise above yourself on all occasions that can cause you sorrow by means of a most ardent love.

(*The soul will receive many favors and consolations when it perseveres in the practice of aspiration.*) However, this is only the entrance to true love. The soul must first of all be tried and purified in the fire of countless sharp trials, deprivations, miseries, abandonments, languors and spiritual deaths. During these trials, the faithful soul avoids seeking consolation in the senses. It follows the path cut out for it. Living in inward tranquility and joy, it desires to be a living and continual holocaust before God, its Beloved, in constant, cruel deaths. But this should in no way frighten the soul or discourage it from running enthusiastically in the lists of love, along with all the true and faithful lovers of God, as long as he is quite pleased with it. Now if the soul experiences any feeling contrary to this, it should not give in to it. For this would be an insult to its Beloved, who desires its happiness more ardently than it can ever understand.

Finally, the proof of true love for God is the great strength with which the soul lovingly sustains him at its own cost in the various deaths that it must undergo. Although the soul endures them out of love and beyond love, it is not deprived of love. On the contrary, it acts with a manly and vigorous love, which enables it to suffer and work without any light or relish, always and simply inspired by the naked and lively simplicity of its heart's desire. Whoever has arrived at this level of experience, can no longer do otherwise than love in this manner. This is due to the profound and continuous touches of divine love which have been granted to the soul, and to the mutual love that is reciprocally received and bestowed.

(*During work and study*) When the soul is busily engaged in external occupations, in order to recollect itself, it should use simple glances and acts. These, by their power, will draw all the faculties of the soul into their simple and loving Object. Here you have a method for performing every activity, interior or exterior, in a holy manner.

When you are busy with some important external task which

prevents you from exercising an ardent and lively love, turn the work itself into an act of love. Perform it as if it were an act of this same lively and burning love. For this reason, remember to direct very interior, simple and brief glances towards God during your work. If the task is so exacting that it demands all your attention, then directing heart-felt glances toward God at various intervals will suffice. After all, perfection does not consist in feeling the Beloved overwhelming the faculties of his spouse with love. But it does consist in seeing, desiring and cleaving to him without any feeling by means of a simple gaze. This gaze is very naked and far removed from the senses. What I say here also applies to the most perfect souls.

As for the *sciences,* it is very difficult to devote oneself to them without prejudice to divine Wisdom. This is due to the great opposition existing between the one and the other. In itself, divine Wisdom is simple and one. Through this sacred gift the soul too becomes simple. It is reformed in its faculties and disposed to be easily united to God with its whole being. The sciences, on the other hand, bring multiplicity into the soul and make its approach to God very difficult.

Therefore, to preserve this wisdom during the course of our studies, we must have an ardent desire always to adhere to God by a simple and joyful inclination of the heart. Then too, we must always cling to the knowledge and certitude we have that *God exists.* To this must be added the exercise of self-mastery and the practice of frequently uniting our whole being to this God of the sciences and of the virtues. This does not mean that, during actual study, we must always feel God flowing in and out of the powers of the soul, filling them and drawing them to himself. It is sufficient if we do not seek a purely natural delight and satisfaction in our study, or make it our final end. Nor does it mean that the sciences should in no way affect or delight us. Indeed, we may enjoy them with moderation, somewhat like spiritual persons enjoy eating and drinking, that is, more out of necessity and for their well-being, rather than for the pleasure and satisfaction of their senses.

In this as in everything else we must be resolutely obedient

out of love for God, and carefully guard against performing this
or any other task, no matter how laborious, away from God's
presence. Moreover, each task ought to be done with equal care
and in the same spirit with which we make acts of love, which
are inclined to be more interior, savory and simple. For him who
has been touched by an ardent desire to love God, there is no
distinction between interior and exterior. Although the soul, in
spite of itself, may feel greatly distracted by external occupations,
still it must endure this painful conflict. It should make a sacrifice
of itself through brief aspirations launched toward God with all
the heart, at least for the space of an '*Ave Maria*.'

If possible, the soul should act thus every fifteen minutes, depending on its hunger and its degree of love. Even this little delay
will seem like ten thousand days because of the great pain it will
feel at seeing itself occupied with things so opposed to simple and
loving occupation with God. This aspiration or loving inclination
might be worded thus: "Since you wish me to study, O my Love,
I do so and will always do so to know you and love you alone.
I will not study out of love for the sciences, but out of love for
your Wisdom." By means of prayer you will unite yourself as
closely to God as possible. Outside of it you will hardly need to
practice any other aspiration than the one given above. But do
not fail to use simple glances and essential conversions (i.e.,
heartfelt desires).

When we are doing difficult work, it is contrary to common
sense to try to say vocal prayers, especially such as are of long
duration. However, we can pray mentally during such distracting
actions by means of simple aspirations, sighs, or burning glances
quickly launched toward God. This supposes a great recollection
of all the powers in the unity of the spirit. Such a practice, therefore, does not apply to the imperfect, because they are not sufficiently advanced.

Act in such a way that your external actions may not draw
you away from your interior peace and liberty of spirit, or distract
you in your simple and loving occupation with God. During this
time use ardent, simple and loving aspirations, consisting of a

few words that are fervently sent forth with all your heart, like this. "O my Love, what must I do here among men? Ah! How good it is, how good it is to be lovingly, nakedly (*in detachment*) and simply united to you. O my Beloved, I am outside, and yet, I live within. Only a very small part of me, O my Love, is outside. Still this is in accordance with your loving will. But the best part of me is occupied with you and in you, in whom my life, my joy and all my delight are to be found. Oh, that I might be allowed to live truly alone, my Beloved, even as a solitary. This would be my greatest delight. But if your love decrees otherwise, so may it be. However, even under such conditions, may I be lovingly occupied with you in an essential manner by means of loving glances, sighs and laments, and by inclinations expressed in simple, burning words that will transport me wholly into you, my Well-Beloved."

Now, even when you form a very simple aspiration with all your heart, like "O my Love!", that is enough for one occasion. Or, "O my Life! O my All! My dear Spouse! May I love you alone. I sleep in you, but my heart watches without, so as not to disturb me." One of these aspirations uttered on each occasion is enough. Through all these darts of love and countless others that are even more ardent, love will be enkindled within you.

(*Advice to a correspondent*)   Make use of subjects and affections which make you more ardent. In this way you will enter more and more into God, and will lose yourself in him above and beyond the simplest and closest union. This will be as easy for you as breathing. If study and mental work hinder this return to God, it will suffice if you frequently direct the glances of your heart toward him with a gentle, easy and loving inclination. By acting thus, you will preserve, at the very least, a simple cleaving to God and will feel yourself far removed from the senses. Moreover, you will have a strong inclination to desire, do and accept all that is God's will. Then you will be lost in the vast region of those spirits who seek God nowhere else except in the intimate depths of their own being. These souls also seek and find him in the sacred image of our Savior, whom they zealously imitate whenever there is an occasion to practice mortification or detachment. But all this is done without them giving up their customary practice of aspiration.

THIRD STAGE

(*Definition: Through aspiration the soul reaches the 'vivifying life' i.e., a high degree of mystical union.*) This (*union of love*) is achieved by the eminent practice of aspiration, or by simple and essential inclinations which contain, in their highest perfection, all that is comprised in expressed and dilated aspiration. It is realized even better by very simple and lofty glances of the soul. These glances originate in the highest point of the will, which is touched and inflamed with love for the Spouse above the understanding and all that is sensible.

After a while the practice of aspiration becomes sweet and easy. With further progress it becomes very sweet and very easy, because it is practiced by means of simple, burning glances and by brief, essential and wordless longings. This occurs especially during a period of complete absorption which God himself produces along with the cooperation of the active powers of the soul. So effective is this practice that it does not permit anything to come between the soul and its blessed and divine Object, either in its dilated action, or in its simple and loving glances. It keeps the soul always firmly united to him, not permitting it to be separated from him for even a moment.

(*Effects and benefits*) When the soul has constantly and ardently practiced aspirative love according to the four degrees mentioned above,[16] it receives loving caresses from God in greater or lesser number according to its progress. At the same time it receives such ardent and efficacious outpourings of his love that the continual enjoyment of its Beloved produces an ever more ardent desire for him. Finding itself so intimately embraced by him, the soul is at a complete loss as to how to respond to the overwhelming torrent of his love which keeps it dilated in the river of divine delights. In this state of simple and delightful intoxication, the ardent desire and inclination of the soul are increasingly sharpened and excited by the loving embraces of its Spouse. And when it sees all its efforts reduced to nothing by the fire of the divine understanding, it surrenders before the splendor of his ravishing beauty.

Sometimes God knocks gently within the deepest part of the soul. Stirred by this very brief and sudden touch, it is completely renewed within and filled with strength, understanding, love and delight.

As for the impressions, transports, raptures and ecstasies which God himself produces in his beloved spouse, we must leave that to him. He is the Master, and can do whatever he pleases with the the soul, for it is his domain. And the soul, seeing itself so cherished and caressed by his Majesty, ought to bear it and sustain it at any cost. If we had to die of it, would that such a sweet life were followed by an equally sweet death.

In this abyss (*of love*), the soul becomes one with its Well-Beloved to such an extent that it almost no longer has any thought or concern for temporal events. In all things its singular love is its joy and glory, happiness and holiness, and the totality of its infinite Object.

Therefore, he who is lost in love, lives very happily in the image of Jesus Christ, after the example of his most singular life. Such a love is completely lost in the abyss of our dear Savior's divine and vivifying life. For he became man out of love for men, and in order to draw his intimate friends strongly and quickly to himself. It is his desire that they should never be separated from him, but that they should be with him in the whole of himself for all eternity.

If you lovingly ponder this truth, love will penetrate you. It will urge you by its gentle and ready prompting to form the following exclamation, or one like it on this subject.

"O sweet, O ineffable, O most penetrating, profound and incomparable Love! Who can set boundaries and limits for You? I do not say, in you, for that is impossible. But who can measure the external evidences of your love in the holy angels and in saintly men? In them you enkindle such a magnificent flame that they are constantly consumed with ineffable sweetness and delight, O Love most delicious! What can creatures speak of in whom you do not exist, or in whom you live in only an ordinary manner! Where you are concerned, my Love, I am guilty of excess. For consumed as I am by the fire of your Love, I think and feel that all men ought to be as I. But so few dwell within themselves, or if they do, they do it so imperfectly that they are entirely taken up with their own plans and tasks. They are ignorant of the real goodness within them and in you, who are most lovable and worthy of imitation above every personal practice. To you, O Love, we must cleave nakedly by a most simple attention and repose, together with a very simple and constant intention and disposition, so as to think of nothing else.

When the soul has reached this degree, it will see and feel that there is no longer anything else in it but a simple spirit and a very simple inclination, a most simple unity and simplicity of thought; in a word, nothing but a simple essence. For this reason, the soul should be absorbed in it in a very subtle and essential manner, and, as it were, only for a moment by means of frequent, intimate glances. Such glances ought to be very simple and lofty, and contain all that can be said. Thus should it dwell as one who is dead, wholly entombed and lost in the abysmal Essence of Jesus Christ, its most beloved Spouse. Nor should it ever depart from him for any reason whatever, even by the slightest movement of deliberate desire.

Anagogical love is more passive than active, and enraptures the soul in its Spouse, even before its total transfusion[17] and consummation.

(*Method of practice*)   When the soul has arrived at the exalted state of pure love through the practice of the various degrees of aspiration, it sends forth the most ardent glances of love toward its Spouse. These glances now become as frequent as breathing. Whether it is awake or asleep, whether it eats, drinks or converses with others, whether it reads, studies or recites the psalms, it is always performing this work of love. Consequently, the soul is more and more intimately united with its simple and infinite Object, and its entire being is drawn and enraptured in him. Thus does the Beloved deal with his most cherished spouse, in order to lose her irretrievably in him and to crown their happiness. He accomplishes this by pouring out a superabundant torrent of divine delights which impetuously and quite simply inundate all the powers from top to bottom. The soul is entirely carried away by the simple rapidity of the action and submerged in the luxuriant sea of its eternal Origin.

The abundance of this love now causes the soul to possess its beloved Spouse constantly as someone who lives and is, as it were, visible in its own flesh and substance. Taking his interior image, which contains all his beauty and perfections, for its continual occupation, it incessantly sends forth ardent and burning glances of love toward him. If, at times, it can possibly express its love in even a few words, these are such as can be launched forth in a moment. For example, "O my Love! O my delight! O my Life! O my Happiness! O my All!" At other times it will exclaim in lost wonder, "O earth! O angels! O all creatures!" In this condition the soul is unable to express itself on any subject whatever, even when that subject might express the nature and excellence of the divine perfections. The reason for this is that these words, few as they are, are uttered with the most exalted and most eminent love that the soul can enjoy on earth without weakening its life and activity. All these acts of the soul are like so many acts of supereminent[18] admiration for the Beloved, who enraptures it in himself beyond admiration.[19]

(*Speaking of a soul advanced in the mystical life*) He who dwells in this state, or within the fire, dwells in his blessed end, providing he leaves his life and natural operations as such, and follows the divine operation which constantly draws him to itself by means of a subtle and continual gaze. This gaze touches the highest point of the understanding, and makes an ineffable impression on it. There it inspires the soul to gaze upon its blessed and beatific Object.

It is a simple gaze and is withdrawn from the senses, as is God who causes it and the soul who receives and endures it. It joins the soul immediately and constantly to him by a very mystical, simple and savory inclination.

Suffice it to say here that, as long as the soul is actually touched, drawn and ravished by the mystical splendors, this divine Gaze (i.e., *the soul's consciousness of God's gaze*) will henceforth always accompany it. It will continue as long as the soul places no obstacle to it, which, however, it can do quite easily (especially in time of death, i.e., *trial*, and great nakedness). There is danger then that the soul may go back to living in and for itself, living on a purely natural level and seeking its own ease. In this case the divine Gaze will vanish and the soul will no longer be aware of God. On the other hand, when the soul pays careful attention to his divine Gaze, it is continually aware of God and constantly inspired to follow him.

As for the divine Gaze, which remains forever in the soul, exciting and enrapturing it by a very simple and subtle impetuosity, it is nothing else than God himself, above all being and non-being. This divine Gaze transforms the soul by a very spiritual stirring, originating in superessential unity. It causes the soul, thus drawn and stirred, to live no longer in itself and to possess nothing of itself or of created things.

To be sure that the soul is always in God, that it is never distracted from his Gaze, is dead to itself and wholly transformed into God, we give the following rule. When some movement of anguish or passion, whatever it may be, is felt, the simple desire to act and to throw itself into God without any express words will be an assurance to the soul that it has its gaze fixed on God. This inclination is very simple, so simple that the soul doesn't seem to have it. Thus the desire to act and the expressed act will be one and the same thing for it. We have already indicated above the occasion when such a desire may appear. Another such occasion occurs when, through drowsiness, the soul has fallen back upon itself, and fears to be distracted, although it may not be so at all, as we have said. This is quite certain and true. If, by divine permission, some dream influences the body or the imagination during sleep, the soul may ascertain its superessential unity by the practice

of the above-said rule, i.e., checking to see if it has a desire to act
in God, or if this desire has already become an act.

(*Contemplative souls*)   When these souls are not actually ravished
by the powerful and extraordinary attraction of God, their ordinary
practice is to long for God as ardently and essentially as possible.
For them this is almost as easy and ordinary as breathing, because
of the profound habit they have formed in this kind of prayer.

Now there are different kinds of aspiration to suit the needs of
these souls. For those who live more in the senses there are more
simple and remote aspirations. And for those who are completely
God-lost, there are still others. But in all this variety the Holy
Spirit is the Author, Mover and the Master. And so, these souls
and their exalted way of life which produces such an absorbing
and sweet contemplation, are God's delight here on earth.

Thus we see that this practice of ardent love is the way by which
God seeks loving encounters with these souls and they with him.
In them, lover and Beloved are united in intimate and ineffable
embraces, in the inexpressable love and sweetness of the whole
of God. At certain times this is done so frequently that it is a
great wonder how such souls continue to live under the impact of
these most sweet and loving impulses, often very rapid and impetuous.

Be resolved, right in the beginning, not to rest in a multiplicity
of objects, for example, in what appears to be good, beautiful,
perfect, etc. For souls, given to such attachments, seek God only
from the outside and for their own sake, because of the great reward
and the merits they expect from him. But on your part, pay no
attention to external things, which appear to be beautiful and delightful. Remain undivided in all things: simple, dissolved and
lost in naked abstraction.[20] This should not be interrupted. For
it is God who produces it and causes it in you, and you should
always respond to him by maintaining an elevation and practice
in keeping with your state.

As a result, your thought will be changed into affection in order
to produce love and to transform it into an act of remarkable
scope and insight. From it you will receive spiritual impressions

that are most pure and profound, and a thousand times more extensive, simple and tasteful than before. Now, a great and ardent love will enable you to form very simple and wonderful elevations.

In this state the eye of your mind will always be open, and will gaze upon its blessed Object with a simple and joyful inclination, and with a look that is lofty and constant. Your mind, thus illumined by God, will be like a very bright and clear mirror, that reflects the divine image. This image will illumine the whole man exteriorly and interiorly, so as to draw everything wonderfully inward into simple unity, and above all understanding. Your external works and actions, however, will always be done with enlightened discretion and foresight.

But these lofty elevations do not occur, at least not very often, in those who seldom make aspirations. Such souls are content to live indifferently. They pray twice a day, and seldom practice the presence of God in their exercises; when they do, they do it very coldly. So this practice is not for them. But it belongs to those who are strongly drawn by God, and abhor the animal life like death itself. These souls have no desire to be preoccupied with their tasks beyond what is necessary, or, for that matter, with anything below God.

Those who have passed beyond the need for many corporal austerities, rest with great pleasure in God himself, and not in his gifts, or in their ineffable delights, or in anything less than him. They live in God with as much avidity as the fish that feeds on the water which is its element. When they are obliged to perform some task, even if it be manual work, they are not drawn out of him, nor are they filled with forms and images. Their interior repose remains undisturbed. At all times they keep the eye of their understanding open to look with admiration and pleasure upon him who draws them to himself. At the same time the heart too is kept open by the imperceptible action of this intellectual and loving inclination, as well as by a simple and almost continual movement. Thus the heart is united to God by very subtle acts and movements of love, admiration and wonder over the infinite nature of God. In an ineffable manner, they see him in his own unity as an inscrutable and impenetrable abyss, and as a sea having neither depth nor shores. In their exalted elevation they contemplate him beyond all his perfections, which they perceive to be nothing else than himself.

Even though the soul has reached the stage of being completely lost in the infinite abyss of God, nevertheless, as soon as the depths of the soul are opened by the frequent and ardent irradiations[21] of God, the will is smitten with a constant desire to follow what it sees and feels drawing it to itself. When the heart has been more or less strongly touched, it always follows this loving inclination.

(*Souls touched by God, whose interior action is simple, and are drawn by grace to complete inner unity*)   Unity of spirit is accomplished quite simply and, as it were, remotely by an easy, active and more or less elevated converse which draws the soul inward by its efficacious action. Here the acts of the soul become simple and one. It has no need of any special converse. For the subtlety of its glances, and the simplicity of its gaze surpasses all the converse that the soul could ever devise, in order to be drawn and dilated inwardly. This secret elevation and attention is called *anagogic*, because it carries the soul beyond converse by its simple and subtle influence. Moreover, it draws and dilates the soul by a pure and efficacious light which gives it a pleasant satisfaction. This pleasure is not to be despised, because it is meant to draw the soul inward and to dilate it.

(*During prayer*)   Since the soul ought to be alone and onefold in its complete return to the fathomless and shoreless sea of its eternal Origin, it should, therefore, devote itself solely to God, direct its attention to him, and not give up until it is completely lost and poured out into him. Consequently, when it must sing the Psalms in public, love, or, to speak more correctly, its Spouse will easily teach it how to long for him, and pour itself out into him. The sense of every verse will encourage it in this practice, and will inspire it to send forth looks and supereminent longings to God. This ardent manner of acting eminently and essentially contains all that could ever be said or written of the praises and grandeurs of its Spouse. It seems to be almost the last stage of the soul's active desire in its unique Object. This manner of aspiring to God does not permit any distinction between one occasion and another, between one day and another, or between what is good and what is better. It is also free from a multiplicity of practices. Thus the soul advances steadily in ardent aspiration which draws and ravishes it wholly out of itself into its eternal, infinite and un-created Object.

In order to dilate itself in prayer and aspire to God wherever it may be, the soul may use the aspirations which I have written elsewhere. However, I do not wish to imply that he, who uses them, should strive to produce a multitude of confused acts. Some think that, if they do not act thus, they are not loving as they should. It is a very common fault among those who are in the practice of love. It is sufficient if they are not interiorly idle for any notable length of time, especially when the soul has com-pletely returned to itself. But if it is truly touched by love and loves ardently, its active love will not allow it to remain idle.

Moreover, if the state being considered here is sufficiently and perfectly acquired, and becomes an easy and an effective habit, it stands above every distinction of good, better and best, and above a multiplicity of exercises. Here the soul gives itself up to a loving, simple and unique occupation, above every private and particular exercise. It draws all things above every exercise and reduces them to simple unity of spirit. In this unity the Spouse alone is sufficient for it and the soul in reciprocation strives to please him by its generous and constant fidelity. It lives by him, for him and in him alone. In every trial and difficulty, it says to him from the deepest center of its ardent love "You belong to me, my Love, and I belong to you. What you are for yourself, you are also for me. Whatever the cost may be, I belong to you forever. O blessed spirits sing out a new canticle of infinite praise, because your Spouse is my Spouse. By the power of his infinite love he lives by me, for me and in me, as I live by him, for him and in him."

When you are very dry and feel the absence of your divine Spouse, return to making aspirations. But do not become uneasy if they seem to be ineffective and wanting in savor. That is due to the suspension of your active powers. If this suspension is complete, as will often be the case, so that you are forced to die cruelly in a state of inaction, then remain content and tranquil within yourself, or better yet, in your Spouse. Look at him attentively and with a steady gaze, in spite of the great efforts and cruel sorrows that you must endure. Endure them, however, not in yourself, but in him. Although you may seem to be suffering outside of him, and it may look as though he has completely abandoned and rejected you, be very careful not to believe this. But, with a living and deep faith, hold to the truth of God's presence and constant assistance. This will give you some relief in your sufferings. It will also make your soul strong, unshaken and tranquil in enduring the severe trials of the Spouse's apparent absence.

Do not begin to utter cries of complaint and distress with an impulsive or even a pronounced effort of your active powers. That would be dangerous and would produce the greatest darkness in you. You must gently direct the simple and essential glances of your soul to God, longing and grieving for the presence of your divine Spouse from the sheer depths of the soul. Always and in everything desire his perfect pleasure. So, with a humble and patient love, wait for his much desired return, and believe that this state is more beneficial for you than you think. For it is only in this way that you will convince your Spouse that you are really faithful.

(*Addressed to a soul in the transforming union*) If you have passed into the abyss of charity and have been transfused into the divine Essence, you will, so to speak, feel neither yourself nor God. You will be unable and unwilling to form simple aspirations, which supposes explicit action. Nor will you be able to form even simple and imperceptible glances. This, too, supposes some ability to act, and, consequently, implies a certain lack of union and separation, because the soul uses this method in order to transform itself more perfectly into the essence of the Spouse.

When you reach a certain degree of love, you will be inclined more to look at and simply to contemplate your divine Object, rather than to speak or to make acts. For to what purpose do we make such efforts, if not in order to elevate ourselves by means of God's persuasive assistance? And if your soul is already elevated, either by God's penetrating and loving touch alone, or together with our efforts, what need is there then for multiplying our acts?

Once you have acquired this wonderful habit of love, you will feel yourself wholly transformed and lost, for love will penetrate into the deepest depths of your being. Here you will feel that you have so much to see and taste in height, breadth, length, depth and simplicity, that there will be no need at all to raise yourself up to this level by any acts of love on your part.

Thus the soul is raised above all its efforts, to a state of simplicity and a lofty contemplation of God. Quite often it feels a repugnance for using its own activity, due to the simple, naked and delightful thought of the Beloved which then binds the soul under the spell of its gentle action. For God who is here contemplated in a lofty and naked manner, does not demand any other activity of the soul except certain simple aspirations. These suffice to keep it quietly occupied and peacefully at rest in God, its sovereign Good, beyond the many ardent aspirations that it might otherwise form for this purpose.

Now the reason for such repugnance of spirit is that the soul has become more simple, and has been raised to a more lofty spiritual level, and would not know how to continue in this state for any length of time by means of its own activity. Therefore, in this struggle, or, better to say, opposition, it is sufficient if the soul, from moment to moment, forms a few very ardent acts of love. For it should be content rather to look and contemplate, to be dissolved and to delight in gazing upon its Beloved, than to carry on a most affectionate converse. So the soul must be determined to contemplate its infinite Object, far removed from all forms and images.

At this stage, contemplation becomes a science without science. It needs no means and is possessed without wonder;[22] but the return from it is wonder. It is the action and effect of the Divine Spirit, drawing and enrapturing the human soul into itself. Thus

it becomes eminently recollected in exalted unity. Quite often it is
so deeply penetrated and stirred by the touch of love that it feels
dissolved and completely transformed in the vast sea of fiery love.
There it sees itself so deeply plunged into this fire that it becomes
the same thing with it and in it, as well as one and the same life,
both in living as well as in dying.

Nevertheless, even though this state is evidence of a singular
blessing and progress, the soul must not remain for too long a
time without using its own activity. However, this activity should
not be too immersed in the senses or in oneself. Rather should it
be spent in making simple exclamations, laments and affectionate
resolves to imitate Jesus Christ constantly and ardently. Finally,
with the help of this continual gaze, it should imitate him on
every occasion whether the demand is great or small, in order to
develop a pure, perfect and exalted love.

(*The converse of the soul with God in the mystical marriage*)
"My Beloved, You understand me well, since I express myself
sufficiently in simple, solitary sighs, inclinations and glances.
Through them I am transported into you easily and subtly with
the speed of lightning.

(*To a correspondent*)   If you do not have the strength to form
frequent acts (*of aspiration*), practice the exercise of simple inclination, by directing frequent looks, laments and sighs toward God.
This practice comes more from the heart than from the senses.
In your case I believe you already possess it as an established
habit. However, you must keep it vigorously alive by lovingly
renouncing yourself at all times. The soul makes better acts and
advances more quickly by acting according to the spirit rather
than according to the senses.

(*In Trial*)   Those who are in this state (*viz. of pure love*), whether
they be beginners (*in it*), proficients, or even perfect, are not
sinless. On the contrary, the Beloved takes great pleasure in testing
the souls of his spouses in various ways. This he does by means
of their faults (which are not indeed serious faults, but such as

spring from ordinary human frailty), lest they exalt themselves and become inflated with pride and self-love, over what they have received from him and are in him. He loves them better with their faults, not simply because of their faults, but because of what they produce, namely, a profound humility, self-denial, uprightness and steadfastness in pure and loving union with him. You may be sure that he would not allow them to fall, if it were not for this reason. For his Majesty, who desires only his glory in this kind of treatment, wishes to be gratified in these conflicts by the renunciation and self-denial of his spouses.

Therefore, it is the duty of the faithful soul, who desires solely to please its Spouse, to give him this much desired pleasure, by rising up from its faults and extraversions with the same love, as if it had not fallen, and continue its aspirations. It need only say to him, "O my Love and my Life! To what have I come? I have been lured away and have taken delight in myself. Ah! What have I done? I have made myself unlike you. Pardon me this offense, O my Love. With the help of your grace, it will never happen again." Even if it should fall many times each day, it must always rise up in this manner with full, certain, and loving confidence in its divine Spouse.

This practice is important and the renunciation demanded here is keen and profound. For the soul should know that its renunciation ought to be such that it will always accomplish its purpose on these occasions, in the most pure, spiritual and isolated part of the soul, which is pure spirit. This pure and simple renunciation consists in being completely detached from self in a state of non-action and non-willing (*complete indifference*), whether to live or to die, without seeking self in the least possible way. That is easy to say, but the practice of it seems unattainable.

Would that we could really find souls so faithful to their Spouse, that, as far as they were concerned, they would remain forever unknown to men when it was a question of their vindication, or of sufferings that affected their ordinary comfort! However, we must not understand this to mean that they may never reveal themselves to their superiors, especially when the latter inquire about their feelings in their trials.

Therefore, in order to persevere in its fidelity, the soul must not pay attention to what it feels, but to what it desires. It should endeavor to keep the depth of the heart solidly and perfectly fixed in its accustomed course of action, in an ardent desire to love for the sake of love itself, and in gazing upon its Spouse within. For it is he who then commands within the spirit, as he subtly and almost imperceptibly draws all the powers of the soul to himself. And so the soul should keep a simple attention fixed upon its interior, as it turns to the divine Spouse with open heart. The practice of this truth is so important that every loving soul, who observes it faithfully and constantly, will always meet with the complete approval of its Spouse.

1. Since John of St. Samson is a recognized master in the art of aspirative prayer, this chapter contains all that he wrote on the subject, at least in his published works. For a more contemporary explanation of the prayer of aspiration, readers may read **Union With the Lord in Prayer** by Rev. Venard Poslusney, O. Carm., Living Flame Press, Box 74, Locust Valley, New York, cf. pp. 14-19.

2. These titles and sub-titles were added by the translator in order to give an intelligible organization to the material. Phrases in italics and in brackets are also additions of the translator.

3. This phrase is taken from Ruysbroeck and applies to the first stage of the spiritual life known as the beginners stage.

4. I.e. those whose religious experience is only a matter of emotions, but does not change their will or their behavior.

5. The word 'hate' should be understood in the sense in which it was used in Jn 12:25, i.e., he who would follow Jesus must hate even himself, viz. to discipline, detach and deny his body appetites, his desires in order to bring them into control and into the service of Christ. But we must also admit that as part of the culture of the times, this 'hatred' was sometimes carried too far. We must heed the wise advice of St. Teresa of Avila who encourages us to take care of the body, so that it may perform many good services for the soul. But she does not excuse us from the universal call to detachment from all things that would hinder our union with Christ.

6. I.e., feelings that we have in common with all animal and sense life; e.g., body appetites, emotions of fear, hatred, joy, love, etc.

7. Here John depends on Henry Herp who gives a detailed explanation of each of these four degrees in his **Speculum Perfectionis,** chap. 46. It is worth giving in detail. In the **first degree,** Herp writes, the soul should generously **offer** God all he asks by his inspirations, especially perfect self-denial and contempt of self, detachment from all sense pleasures, even though they are small things, such as useless conversations, and associations, idleness, curiosity, mortification of the natural passions, such as inordinate joy, sorrow,

love, fear and even vain hope; promptly and willingly to bear every adversity for God's sake; freely to offer self to bear all that God wishes. In the **second degree** the soul should not only ask to receive everything that God has, but also all that God is. Above all to ask for naked love in order to enjoy God alone in his immense, naked love, for man may not enjoy anything so as to put in it his final repose, except God alone. The soul should also ask to know the good pleasure and will of God most perfectly in order to fulfill it more perfectly; and a perfect knowledge of self in order to despise and humiliate it; also perfect knowledge of all the virtues and the grace to acquire them; a constant desire to grow in love, like spiritual breathing in order to keep alive in love. To ask for many useful things, both for soul and body. In the **third degree**, the soul should gather all its imperfections in one bundle and cast them into the immense fire of divine love; it should be filled with burning desires. With ardent longings it should ask the Beloved to clothe it with his virtues, i.e., those of Christ. It should seek to **conform** its life to that of Christ in all his perfections, especially in the virtues of his humanity. In the **fourth degree** the soul seeks to **unite** and pour out its will into the will of God. This will must be the soul's ultimate desire and joy, no matter how difficult things are interiorly: e.g., withdrawal of grace, devotion, consolation, darkness, rebellion of senses, temptations, etc., or exteriorly: e.g., persecution, detraction, confusion, sickness, mockery, etc. At this time the soul should be confident that all comes from God and is meant to prove its fidelity; afterwards he will reward it with divine gifts and graces. This leads to the state or degree of fervent love (**6th degree of love**). Here the soul is carried above itself by ardent love, but at once falls back because of its natural heaviness. This degree arises from a certain loving contest between God and the soul. Thus the powers of the soul become very energetic and active as they adhere to God, directing all its knowledge and affection to God so that it seems no longer to use its external senses, as it were asleep. The loving soul then says, "I sleep according to the external man, and my heart watches, namely, with my Beloved whom I hold enclosed in my heart."

8. Cf. glossary.

9. Cf. glossary.

10. Cf. glossary.

11. Cf. glossary.

12. Very likely he means a loving gaze, not necessarily expressed in words.

13. I.e., simple or simplified aspiration composed of a few words, or simple glances and heartfelt desires which are capable of lifting up the soul entirely into God. Cf. glossary.

14. John also uses this term to mean ordinary meditation together with affectionate converse with God. (cf. **Carmelus**, p. 204, by Janssen)

15. I.e., by mortification of the senses.

16. Cf. p. 11.

17. Cf. glossary.

18. Cf. glossary.

19. Cf. glossary.

20. Cf. glossary.

21. Cf. glossary.

22. Cf. glossary.

CHAPTER III

CONTEMPLATION

(*Proximate Dispositions*)   When the soul receives the secret and sensible anointing of the Holy Spirit, it is drawn into God in such a simple and lively manner that it is already to some extent beyond those discourses which explain the divine grandeurs and perfections. At the same time, it feels that it is above all created things. They leave such an insipid impression on its spirit that it experiences repugnance for them, as if they were something beneath its feet, or to put it better, as if they did not even exist. This state is an elevation to a certain simple unity of spirit which produces repose and a simple, naked contemplation of God. While the understanding contemplates him with a simple eye, it is deeply penetrated by frequent lights and divine touches.

This in turn makes various impressions on heart and soul which are above sensible discourse. The interior action suitable for such a state is savory and secret, and is far more spiritual and essential than it is sensible. It is above the considerations which the soul is accustomed to make in order to raise itself up to God, even when they concern divine love. This state and its interior activity consists in a simple and naked glance of the soul which, while keeping the eye of the understanding open, needs only a very simple and imperceptible effort to remain active. Thus the soul follows this attraction, aided by a very spiritual light, which completely surpasses what is sensible. In its nakedness it is more concerned with continually looking at its Object than with speaking to him. For it sees and feels quite clearly that its discourses rather withdraw it from him than bring it to him. Now, when it is being subtly moved and influenced, it feels that it is in an entirely new region other than that of the senses, namely, in the region of pure and simple spirits. The region of the senses, with its sensible love, considerations, meditations and instructions, is below this state. Thus the soul no longer needs to be occupied with these matters, nor even with the virtues as virtues. It needs only a simple and naked love to satisfy it.

In certain souls, all this takes place more by means of the diverse irradiations[1] and splendors of the divine attractions, than by meditations which are meant to dispose the heart and interior faculties for the divine touches. So many splendors, and such subtle and secret knowledge have been repeatedly revealed to the soul by these divine attractions, that it finds it impossible to express any part of it. These souls have only one word to describe the experience, *ineffable*. From this we can see that they are raised above those analogies that men devise in order to know God in the first stages of mystical knowledge.

This way of prayer is certainly good, secure and excellent. It is better than those methods of prayer which depend on the senses, and require constant activity on the part of the soul. Therefore, the soul must follow God with a humble confidence and without fear of deception. A constant proof that it is not deceived may be found in the fact that its love is in no way contrary to its actual interior state. Moreover, in the greatest difficulties, this love needs only itself. It has no need of reasoning, for that is inferior to it. It rises above all this by a simple and naked gaze upon its infinite Object.

Therefore, when such a soul is contradicted by the judgments of men, it believes it has found what it was looking for, namely, an opportunity to exercise its love externally in imitation of our Savior, who similarly manifested his love in more than thirty years of labor. It looks at him constantly and is in continual admiration at his goodness, mercy and the marvelous manifestations of his divine love. It sees how he went forth from the Father's bosom and descended to earth, clothing himself with our humanity in order to make us God by adoption and participation. This is enough to keep its spirit constantly ravished in him. Vile and miserable as it is, it feels that a thousand lives would not be suffi-

cient to give in return for such magnificent love. But since we
are made in his image and he in ours, he has an infinite love for us,
in spite of our weakness and poverty. For it is he who gives us
the dispositions necessary for love and the graces to bring it to
perfection. On our part we accomplish this by the constant praise
which we give him.

We must strive for this perfection with an ardent desire. And
when we have attained it, we must continue in it by conforming
our life completely to that of our Savior. Now to do this as it
ought to be done, nothing is so necessary as patient suffering. It is
a war of love. And the happiness of loving souls in this life consists in sustaining it with complete peace of mind and heart, and
with the greatest delight. This, however, will not take place until
we are interiorly dead to all things. For as long as we feel a repugnance for anything, it is a sign that our heart is not full of God,
and our soul is not completely subject to him.

Therefore, we must constantly die to our repugnances. And even
if they last a lifetime, we must endure them joyfully. For it is
in this that our perfection then consists. And it is worth more
in this life than the enjoyment of God's secrets, lights and transports. The transports of the will are far better for the soul than
the transports of the understanding, for the latter are subject to
great illusion and deception.

Actually, the state we have described is itself a kind of transport, since it attaches the soul to God as to someone who is continually seen, although imperfectly. For the simple eye of the
understanding, which is only partially illumined is opened for naked
contemplation. In such contemplation the divine Spirit ravishes
and draws the lower man entirely to himself, and is delighted
beyond description. In this state the soul feels the weight of external
crosses quite keenly, but that isn't important. It is not interested
in seeing or knowing who is to blame for the blows it receives.
For it is very certain that they come from the fatherly hand of
God. It is convinced that such crosses are very necessary in order
to keep it faithful in its love for God.

(*Letter no. 6: advice*)   Be tranquil, simple and faithful to the constant gaze upon your Object. Do not abstain from transitory things at the wrong time. They should not influence you, for you ought to be truly dead, in order to live in the constant contemplation of God, outside of the senses, above the work of the intellect and beyond admiration. Become so simple and tranquil, through a moderate mental control, that you do not allow your mind to be divided ever so little by any imaginary notion. When you become aware of these divisions, reject them, but without making formal acts. Instead, exercise a restraining influence by cultivating a very simple desire for God. For you that will be an act without act, and yet it will have a very simple effect. But if some passion or temptation should take an inordinate hold of you, it is for God, who is, to dispel it when it will please him, and not you, who are not. Thus it is God, so to speak, who endures it in you. Therefore, it is for him to do with it whatever he pleases, without your being otherwise excited over it. (*Note: John of St. Samson is talking to a soul advanced in virtue, and therefore, very spiritual and fervent, not lax and tepid. From the tenor of the first part of the letter, this soul seems to be enjoying mystical prayer.*)

(*Not all receive the grace of contemplation.*)   I admit that the grace of lofty contemplation is not given to everyone. And it is even less necessary to be lost in such a marvelous state of love. But if a man is to be reformed, he must at least acquire all the virtues to a considerable degree. And, since it is necessary to be occupied in God and with God in order to attain to the virtues, every soul must of necessity practice this occupation if it wishes to attain the holiness that is necessary for it. What pleasure, I ask you, can God take in a man who is immortified in his desires and actions, and constantly seeks himself in a life that is entirely animal? I say, *animal*, because, to live in this life without being conscious of God is to live like a beast, and in constant sin.

(*Speaking of those who know only the active life and do not wish to rise higher:*)   Men know nothing better and do not think that others can do anything better. In this they judge others by themselves, without considering the extraordinary assistance of God. Such an attitude comes from the fact that no one wants to surpass himself, because of the innumerable labors he must undertake in order to arrive at perfect love of God. Many begin and then suddenly give up. They are discouraged by the struggles and combats which they must generously endure in order to become absolute masters of themselves. They cannot accept a life that is a constant holocaust to God. This fact makes us justly deplore such an appaling misfortune. For everyone ought to be perfect in the virtues, and these are acquired by love. They ought to have a hatred for sin, even venial sin, and live in a complete and wholesome charity without injury or stain.

(*Imperfection in contemplative souls*) As for imperfection, which can exist in this divine way (*viz. contemplation*), it comes more from the newness of the experience than from any deliberate design. For, since the spouse is new in this exercise of love, all its powers are affected in such a delightful and penetrating manner that it often goes to excess, and indulges in gestures which pass for great imperfections in the eyes of onlookers. But they ought to be attributed more to the abundance of the spirit, which strongly dominates them, than to any voluntary immortification. However, some disorder may be present. But anyone who knows the state of such souls very easily pardons such faults, knowing that, in the abundance of such great delight, love is not easily controlled. In this manner certain souls become quite spiritual.

When a soul has passed completely into God, it doesn't seem to have much holiness. But actually it is as elevated in holiness, as its state is infinitely elevated above the elementary stages of the spiritual life. The splendor of it shines forth marvelously in all the soul's actions, words, gestures and feelings, to the great edification of its neighbor. For anyone who is disposed by virtue to seek this state, all this clearly manifests the Spirit of God, who fills these souls with abundance. He rules them firmly, inflames them ardently, and enlightens them exceedingly. Still I know well of what I ought to complain, although I know not of whom. Hence, I complain of all by saying, that I have hardly ever known or will know anyone who remains steadfast and generous in the vexations of nature, even in time of necessity, and much less on occasions of free choice. On such occasions, the soul gives up what is right and good for what is expedient. At the first and slightest encounter with such vexations, the vanquished soul descends from its cross, and runs for consolation to the senses.

This fact convicts certain spiritual persons of great weakness. If the trials of nature last for some time, they cannot bear the agony in a spirit of naked love. Yet, when they are delivered from these sieges, they say wonderful things about them in order to encourage others to perfection. But at the same time it is quite evident that they have only a theoretical knowledge of these trials, not a practical experience. For this mortal agony and the prospect of its length makes them turn their back on God at the first shock. This is what I greatly fear in my own case. For I consider him, who is faithful to God in these trials, a phoenix upon this earth. Nevertheless, it is true that there are souls who serve God even to this stage of constant death. If we do not recognize them, let it suffice us to know that there are actually some souls who are cherished by God even to that extent, so that they might imitate him constantly in naked and essential love.

Love, when it reflects too much upon itself, very often turns its subject into a dreamer. Thus the soul becomes a slave to the imagination, even though it is more or less spiritualized, living more by its dictates than by naked faith, and thus bringing great injury to God and harm to itself. For this reason, many only give themselves to God by halves, depending on the occasion and the circumstances—a thing greatly to be deplored. For if ordinary men saw and knew the great excellence of the ways of the spirit, and could live in this unknown region, ah Lord, what would they not say of such souls!

(*Description of Contemplation*) The mystical way as such is totally contrary to the scholastic (*which rises to the knowledge of God by going from the visible to the invisible and intellectual, and thus to God himself, and by these means attains to the love of God.*) If it uses considerations in the beginning, it does so in such a way that they may be an aid to the will. Ordinarily, it sets aside such considerations, and proceeds to inflame the will with all kinds of affections, especially such as have been more recently produced by consideration. The affections of souls in the mystical way succeed each other and are united very much like the links of a chain. The first affection is developed and expanded according to normal practice. From there the soul goes on to another affection and then to another, and so forth, according to the fervor of its desire. These affections, thus enchained, arise out of the virtues, or out of love which is the inspiration, master, sanctifier and the all of the moral virtues.

The mystical way (i.e., *the way of contemplation*) ought to be, with good reason, the way that is followed by all men who are chosen to know God and to love him perfectly, and not the other way (i.e., *the scholastic way*), which we have shown to be a real obstacle and hindrance to the former. But what can we do? Men are so full of their own self-love, and therefore, are in such darkness that God cannot approach them, so to speak, in order to enlighten them with his extraordinary and vivifying ray.

But those who are chosen by his Majesty for such an exalted state, give more glory to God in this world than people imagine. It is in this state that the soul very soon learns the mystical science, although what it can say of it is nothing in comparison with its great eminence. Here the soul is clothed with God and all his qualities as with a vestment. Here it is learned and completely filled with divine inspirations. God comes incessantly into the soul, and the soul reciprocally goes to God with all its heart. Finally, its entire being is here transfused into the eternal sea.

But the soul dwells in its inmost center, or rather God dwells in it. And there it steadily contemplates him with a very ardent, simple and lively gaze. For souls who are very perfect in their supereminent state, this gaze is very subtle, and keeps them deeply recollected in God. But as I have said, this is what the ordinary person thinks of least, whereas souls thus favored, think only of God, whom they see, and God, on his part, continually inspires them to seek only his pleasure both in their interior and exterior actions. Thus they live lovingly beyond love, although not without love. On the contrary, it is a life lived in infinite love.

When you have acquired this excellent habit of love (i.e., *of pure, spiritual love*) you will feel completely absorbed by it as it penetrates deeply into the center of your being. There you will be conscious of enjoying a taste and a gaze of such height, breadth, length, depth and simplicity that you will attain this state quite easily, without any effort on your part.

Thus the soul is elevated to an exalted gaze and contemplation of God that is beyond its own effort. In fact it often feels a repugnance for its own activity, because of the sweet influence exerted on it by this simple, naked and delightful thought of God. And God, who is then contemplated in such a lofty and naked manner, does not ask anything more of the soul than simple acts of love. These suffice to keep it occupied and fixed in him, so that it has no need to form many fervent affections.

The reason why the soul feels repugnance for activity is that it is more simple and is elevated to a higher state, and it would not be able to continue in this state if it carried on a vigorous and long drawn out activity. Therefore, it is sufficient if, at intervals, it forms certain intimate acts of love. Meanwhile, it should be determined rather to look at and to delight in the sight of its infinite Love, than to carry on a very affectionate conversation. Hence, the soul must remain fixed between time and eternity, as it contemplates its infinite Object, far above every form and image.

Contemplation at this stage becomes a science without science, and does not use methods. The soul possesses it without wonder,[2] and returns from it with admiration. Therefore, I say that contemplation is the action and the effect of the divine Spirit drawing, elevating and ravishing the human spirit to itself. In this Spirit, the soul is profoundly recollected in great unity. Often too, it is so deeply penetrated by a touch of love that it feels as though it were melted and completely transformed by the immense sea of fire which consumes it. It is so plunged and absorbed in this fire that it constantly becomes the same thing with it and in it, as well as one life with it.

Still, even though this state brings great advantage to the soul, it would be well for it not to remain for too long a time without returning to its own activity. However, this action should not be carried on too much in the senses or in oneself, but, as it were, by simple aspirations, laments and affectionate resolutions to imitate Jesus, our divine and human Model, constantly and fervently.

(*Attractions of God should be followed.*)   Since these souls, my Beloved, will be raised to a high degree and moved by the influence of your love beyond their own action, they will be obliged to follow you with simple resignation. At this time they must look at you with profound, simple and naked admiration, as long as the attraction lasts, without seeming to do anything. To act otherwise would be to place an obstacle to you and your gifts. Such action would cloud your light and the soul would become sensibly dark by resorting to its own activity. This would be a very serious drawback. These souls should notice, my Beloved, that what I am saying here supposes a strong divine attraction. For it is one thing to be strongly and ardently touched and raised to abundant savor and light, and another thing to be touched and raised only subtly and remotely. This second kind of attraction should be followed with a gentle and moderate activity. Facility in doing this is called the practice of prayer, in contrast to the painful and laborious work of meditation made by using the understanding. In the latter exercise, when the understanding is sufficiently enlightened, then the will applies itself to the same subject for its own nourishment.

Now, I am going to speak of another practice, my Beloved, in which the soul will find it easy to gaze upon you steadily with the eye of its understanding. This faculty contemplates you without images, until the soul feels a descent in its elevation. Then it returns to the practice of making its own acts, stopping occasionally to contemplate you. Thus the soul passes the time with ease, pleasure and relish in tranquil exercise. In these experiences however, it should not reflect upon itself, but should return all to you as a gift. For you only grant it favors that it may return them to you for your great glory. Concerning your stronger touches and attractions, which seem rather to transport the powers than to draw them by their own effort, they are an excellent, quick and delightful form of contemplation which is not easy to describe. In this state, my Beloved, you want the soul to follow you quietly, and thus happily allow itself to be directed into the divine region according to the influence of your attraction. The soul should then remain alone, looking at you with ineffable delight, wholly liquified in the fire of pure love, or in the pain of loving compunction. The difference in these delightful elevations consists in the effect of your first coming into the soul, which is more or less penetrating and abundant, depending on its life and interior state. Once it has attained them, it receives great profit from them. For, as the number of your comings grow, your blessed touches fill it with new gifts and riches, and consequently, with a marvelous splendor and adornment, both in virtue as well as in love.

The practice of what I am discussing here, my Beloved, becomes more and more pleasant and ineffably delightful. For the soul is finally completely possessed by you, and, as it were, drowned in you. Now, it enjoys infinite delights, poured out with abundance. In proportion to its different elevations it is wonderfully renewed and entirely changed into you. These elevations occur first in the sensitive and inferior part of the soul. Their number cannot be easily conceived, except by those who are very holy and masters in the theory of this divine science. But, my Love, this entire ascent is not absolutely necessary in order to be very holy and perfectly loving. It is sufficient if the soul does all it can when you first bestow your holy attractions upon it. It should use them in order to rise above sensible things, and to become pure and free of all created images and figures. Insofar as it is free to do so, it should earnestly apply itself to this task. Thus it will disengage the various spheres of its nature and will gradually become spiritual without being aware of it. And in due time, it will find itself influenced by affections that are more elevated, simple and ardent.

After these attractions, the soul experiences poverty, languor, misery, darkness, weakness and similar afflictions. These it endures without, in any way, giving up its spiritual state, a state that is infused as well as acquired. If the soul bears these trials generously, what glory will be yours, my Love, and what profit for the soul! But it can only do this by constantly directing ardent and heartfelt affections to your Majesty, which are beyond all reflection.

(*The divine gaze is God acting in the soul.*) This gaze can only be understood by God himself, the source of it, who draws and raises the soul up to himself. It belongs entirely to God. The soul has a part in it only insofar as it suffers the action of this divine gaze in the highest point of its spirit, while being elevated and transformed into God. Indeed we ought to say it is God himself, rather than some particular work of his. For just as the infinite God comprehends himself whole and entire in his supreme fullness while being supereminently distant from all fullness, so does he comprehend himself through himself in the soul whom he elevates and transports as he draws its gaze by his own (*gaze*). He does this so that it will never more be separated from the nature of God, as the intellectual nature is removed from that which is infinitely above all created nature. Here the soul dwells in God beyond all perception.

(*How to avoid spiritual idleness.*)   If the soul's interior gaze is sufficiently ardent and penetrating, it will not have to form long drawn out acts. At this time, they are contrary to its heart's desire. It already has something better than that. But when it notices that it is able to do so, it should form prolonged and dilated acts. For without such vigilance and exercise of its own acts, the soul would run the risk of being spiritually idle.

If the will has a pronounced dislike for making these acts, this is a clear sign that it does not need them. And the reason is that its interior gaze is strong enough to keep it attentive and recollected in the contemplation of its Object, God. But if this gaze is not something acquired through long practice, it will only be brief and passing, and therefore, will only enable the soul to contemplate its Object for a few moments. However, if the soul has been busy making colloquies, and then feels drawn by its Object, it ought to recollect all its powers in unity, and fix an attentive gaze upon him. But when this gaze grows weak and the soul falls back upon itself, it should begin to make its own acts. In adopting this procedure, it will avoid a deceptive idleness much to be feared here. For there are many lazy souls, who take appearances for the truth. Because they have occasionally experienced a sweet and strong attraction which raised them above sensible things to the contemplation and enjoyment of God, they now consider themselves permanently fixed in this state. But actually it lasts only for a certain time. During this time they need only to follow the gaze by which they are drawn. On such occasions they may use ardent words, such as I have indicated elsewhere, or hidden and subtle sighs of love. These latter come easily to the soul that has become spiritual, due to the divine infusions it has received. Over a long period of time, they have entirely penetrated it with love and light. But once the soul becomes fully conscious of itself, it must once more form its own acts with a wide open heart.

In order to dilate[3] the heart, we should consider God's infinite love for man: how he made the world and created us out of love and for his love. Certainly a marvellous thing and a great wonder! This love is revealed to us in all that we see, hear and possess. They are like so many voices that urge us to love him as our eternal Beginning and Final End, in the enjoyment of whom we are completely satisfied with all the fullness of God. But we shall only share his divinity according to the degree of our love for him. It will also depend on how faithful we are in dying to self and in a constant and living imitation of our Savior.

Therefore, when the soul is left to itself, it should fall back upon its own effort and use the means and the method that its love will suggest in this work. In this way it will not always be following the same set routine, such as we find in written meditations. Let it follow the attraction of Divine Love and accomodate its heart to the ardent affections which touch and draw it to its divine Object.

(*State of aridity*)   (*Letter* 46: *How to act in the state of aridity*)
Now is the time to be faithful to God and lovingly put into practice all that you have ever resolved. In my writings I have spoken to you a great deal about *naked* and *essential love*. This is what you must now practice. Generously surrender your life to God in this painful and bitter agony of soul. Bear it with a strong and generous love. True, it is a painful state. But, since there is no truth in man, except insofar as he has the strength and fidelity to sustain God in God himself, beyond the senses, and his own

actual industry, during this time, you must surrender yourself to God as a constant victim through your naked and essential love. Nevertheless, try to recover sensible love, but without making a great effort, not because it is a better state, but because it is necessary for you, since you are still not strong enough to do without it. Nothing is more suitable for recovering it than the practices I have given you. In their breadth and scope, you will find the means of re-entering into your first feelings. For this reason you must not consult other practices, because they may be too rigorous and that would only serve to dry you up even more, and bring greater darkness into your soul. But if you cannot recover sensible love, you must be patient. However, that will not happen, God willing, inasmuch as it is not the order which God ordinarily observes in the conversion of men. Hence, proceed with humble courage and patient resignation, and his Majesty will return to you when you least think of it. He wants you to work faithfully in this pursuit, not in yourself or for yourself, but in him and for him alone. If you are obliged to be more passive than active, always look for breadth (i.e., *that which does not confine the soul but enlarges it*) in order afterwards to re-enter your lost state (i.e., *of sensible love*).

From my writings select subjects for sweet and loving aspiration, but carefully guard against making violent efforts of the heart. If, perhaps, you find nothing that moves you, it doesn't matter. Always meditate on what you will find there. Through your courage, constancy and enduring patience, sensible love will finally enter into the depths of your heart, and bring you consolation. So far you have conducted yourself quite well in your dereliction. Continue in this spirit. Your present state is the entrance to true holiness and will lead you even deeper into the depths of your inmost being. There, every good is to be found both for God as well as for yourself, and you will obtain it in an ever greater degree through the hidden power of God, and your own patient resignation. This resignation is a result of God's work in your soul, and is all the more marvelous and genuine, the more it is unknown to you. Between God and yourself, rejoice in this as much as possible. Do not neglect any of your external duties. If you must suffer in your soul, do not go looking for consolations either in the senses or in creatures. This would be a very great infidelity. Do violence to yourself. When you are unable to do something, arm yourself with good will. Your practices will show you quite clearly what you should do and endure in such combats. Otherwise, you need nothing else, except, perhaps, some advice.

(*Methods of contemplation*) Since there are many who work actively with intellect and will, while being assisted by your grace, you do not leave them for very long at so mean a table Drawing them to yourself, you raise them up and fill them with your Spirit, inspiring them to contemplate you with a very simple and penetrating gaze. This gaze takes in many admirable truths and thoughts at one time, and leads the soul in ardent pursuit of them, so that it loses itself in the greatest depths of your Spirit. Such souls understand and taste the mysteries of your love in so pleasing and delightful a manner, that no comparison can express it. Thus the contemplation of you brings ineffable enjoyment to the mind and heart of your friends.

There is another flight or ascent of the soul to you, my Beloved, called *simple speculation.* It is the immediate step leading to this easy and penetrating contemplation. Such contemplation confines itself to admiration over the insights and secrets that are given to the soul. Once again the soul returns to sweet and simple speculation, thus maintaining an easy spiritual flight within you, while its deepest being undergoes a very subtle and ardent penetration. Again it enters into the most profound and secret silence of the spirit. Then soaring up to you by a very light, quick and penetrating flight, it remains for some time steadily fixed in contemplating your infinite essence and beauty, beyond admiration. But it all ends in admiration. This lasts as long as the attraction of your ravishing love and as long as the soul feels the strength and vigor of your Spirit. When the human spirit becomes conscious of itself through the dispersion of its faculties to forms and images, it returns anew to the speculation of its subject.

Besides speculation, there is another excellent method called the *way of dilated love.* It is very appropriate for transforming the heart with love, and recollecting it in the depths of the spirit. Nevertheless, the soul must leave this way when it has become ardently inflamed. It should then devote itself to contemplating God in himself. But to return to my former subject, I say that there are a great many degrees and differences both of spirit and of light in simple speculation. The more loving it is, the easier and more excellent it becomes. And the more advanced the soul is in the way of the spirit, the more easily it rises to contemplation.

Therefore, besides natural speculation, there are three other ways of speculation. The *first* is more *theological* than mystical, because it speculates on the most abstract and profound truths of theology, and transfers them to the depths of the soul. God often enters into this speculation in order to raise souls up to himself, often to a high degree. The *second* kind of speculation is *simple, loving* and *mystical*. Because it is pure and spiritual, and is done out of pure love, it contains both spirit and life to an excellent degree. It is incomparably more exalted than the first kind of speculation. The *third* is even more excellent than the other two, because the entire soul is occupied in a very simple and spiritual activity. Now there is a great deal more pleasure and facility in dilating love by means of simple aspiration than in speculation about it. Nevertheless, for anyone who can practice it, *simple speculation* is very pleasant. But that only applies to him who is a complete mystic, whose judgment is in agreement with the science of theology. For, ordinarily, this speculation is not so pure and spiritual, nor so free from forms that it is not mixed with some human artifice and cleverness. There is more of it in one person than in another.

Still, when speculation is assisted by an extraordinary touch of God, then it elevates us to God and carries us out of ourselves. And when God encourages it in us to an ever greater degree, we plunge and lose ourselves in the deepest depth of his essence and his absolute beauty. Then we lose ourselves in the abysses of his ideas and most hidden truths. Or else we sink into the whole of his divine Being, transported by his infinite beauty and pleasure, beyond any possible reflection on ourselves. We are not transported by way of the understanding. Therefore, it does not indicate the excellence of the saints to any great extent. But in this state we are forcefully ravished above ourselves, without being alienated from our faculties. Moreover, there is nothing like the way of pure spirit for a soul that has experienced the powerful attractions and touches of God's spirit. For, since he has ravished it to himself and it has responded by flowing back into him with all its strength and love, gradually it becomes thoroughly spiritual, and is ardently inflamed with the fire of his infinite love.

(*Transforming union*)   Sometimes God knocks gently within the deepest part of the soul. Stirred by this very brief and sudden touch, it is completely renewed within and filled with strength, understanding, love and delight. By such frequent touches, God seems to be saying, "Behold me within you. Do not be afraid of losing me." This is so wonderful that the soul's faith in God and its belief in his awareness of it are continually renewed by his inspiring and exciting gaze and by his most delightful and ardent touch. Thus it becomes more and more confident in its Object. While it dies constantly to its own life, it is swallowed up and irrevocably lost in God. Now God lives all alone in it and without it. Henceforth, love no longer lives or acts for itself, but for its infinite Object, God, who lives, acts and suffers in it in all circumstances. In this state the soul lives only the life of God. It has attained a likeness with God which is above that likeness. It has attained to his image in his own original Essence. Here it is entirely transfused[4] in his immense breadth, beyond all description.

If God is to live in us, we must die completely. Since we cannot die physically before the appointed time, we must die in the conviction that we and all things are nothing compared to God. This conviction is especially helpful in furthering mystical death when it is preceeded by the spiritual practice which the mystics call *active* and *passive annihilation*. The annihilation is *passive,* when the soul does nothing but look at God in simple repose. Such action is very appropriately called passive, because the soul does nothing except endure the divine action with courage, joy and repose of spirit.

On the other hand, when the soul is obliged to perform something either interiorly or exteriorly, which is necessary for its
natural or moral well being, and considers it as if it were nothing
and did not exist, the annihilation is *active*. At such a time it is
God who performs the action in the soul, while the soul itself is
only an instrument. And since he does not want the soul to lose
its gaze by infidelity, he passes before its spirit like a flash of
lightning, and manifests himself to it in an admirable manner.
But there are many who hesitate for a long time over this, because
they do not want to lose themselves entirely, nor do they want
to surrender themselves as victims to God.

In this exalted state—already above all means—the soul enjoys
God and rests in him imperceptibly by means of a very hidden
and naked, passive strength. Its influence upon the soul is more
effective than the strength of the preceeding state which produced
a very simple and naked adherence of the subject to the Object.
For here this strength fixes the soul in an enjoyment, repose, and
singular simplicity that are beyond all understanding.

Here the condition of dying constantly is appropriate for the
soul, because, by this means, it follows that which it knows not
and sees not. Due to a very simple gaze that is lost in God, the
soul has an active and joyful inclination which places it in a most
singular and supereminent[5] repose. One infallibly leads to the other.

In this state the soul begins to see God simply, without forms
or images. All that is annihilated along with the soul's own life
in this ardent, superessential[6] center into which it is transfused.
When the soul's active desire is entirely suppressed by the strength
and simplicity of love, it begins to enjoy its Spouse purely in his
essence by means of simple touches. These touches dilate and enlarge it in simplicity in a way that it has never experienced.

This state (*viz., transformation of soul in God*) consists in an
elevation of the spirit above every sense object. The soul is firmly
settled within itself and looks upon God who draws it to a simple
unity and nakedness of spirit. It is called simple idleness, because
the soul, while being passive, enjoys a union of simple repose
which is beyond sensible forms. Whether it is occupied interiorly

or exteriorly in the performance of some action, it enjoys this in a uniform manner.

In this state the soul is in a simple, naked and obscure condition, without even knowledge of God. The spirit is elevated above all inferior light to the state where it is unable to act with its interior faculties, because they are all willingly drawn and fixed by the power of their unique and simple Object, God. They remain fixed in a supereminent view at the highest point of the spirit. All this is accomplished in the depth of the All-incomprehensible in nakedness and obscurity. There, all that is sensible, specific and created is dissolved in unity of spirit, or rather, in simplicity of essence and spirit. Within, all the powers look steadily and attentively upon God, who engages them uniformly in contemplating him. They are quite simply absorbed by the action of his continual gaze which he maintains in the soul, and which the soul mutually maintains in him.

This continual gaze belongs only to the soul that is moved in a purely passive manner. It does nothing but contemplate its Object in a naked, profound and simple enjoyment. And the more the soul is unconscious of it, so much the better is it for the depth and excellence of this state. In short, in this condition, there is neither creature nor created object, knowledge nor ignorance, all nor nothing, word nor name, past, future nor even present; not even the eternal now. All is lost and dissolved in this obscure mist which God himself produces. It is thus that he takes his delight in the souls in whom it pleases him to accomplish this exalted work.

As for the soul thus ennobled and transformed in substance and in superessential light, it must respond with all its being in him whom it sees and who draws it to himself by this simple ecstasy. It should not allow itself to be occupied by natural affairs which are almost continually presented to it by the faculty of reason. Nor should it listen to nature which is always soliciting it to examine and feel its state, and to reflect upon what it sees and what it is. For nature always seeks to attach itself to some object. It is not able continually to detach itself, as is necessary, from the senses and from what is specific and created. But this is necessary if it is to enjoy its Object freely, in a deep and simple peace of mind, together with most secret lights and a most intimate love and delight.

Now if this soul remains faithful, although it may suffer externally, either through the natural restlessness of its faculties, or through its body, these disturbances will only serve to keep it more deeply recollected in its divine and simple gaze. In this, to a certain extent, it enjoys Paradise on earth. But this enjoyment is far greater and more profound when it is able to give its entire attention, and when the faculties are calm. At the same time its response to the Beloved, whom it sees and contemplates, must be complete and enduring. Hence the soul that is blest with such a divine favor ought to plunge itself continually into the abyssal Essence of God by means of a simple and complete attention. For he now enraptures it with himself and for himself, and transports it into himself. The more such a soul feels disturbed by the senses, so much the more ought it to concentrate on constantly contemplating its blessed Object uniformly, nakedly and simply as far as it is possible for a soul elevated to this supereminent state.

It is here that paradise sometimes flows into the soul, and overwhelms it with divine delights. All its powers are filled with simple love and light. So abundant and marvelous is it that it is beyond description. Still there are some souls to whom this has never happened, and never will happen, unless it be at the moment of death. Meanwhile, they are fixed in this state and gaze steadily upon God in himself by means of a simple and naked faith. Like the just, they live by faith even in the midst of their painful deaths.

But there are other souls who enjoy a greater perfection and enlightenment, to whom this paradise is manifested more often, and still others, who enjoy it very often. When thus favored, they are filled with every kind of happiness and perfection, and seem to be entirely overwhelmed by it even to the point of pouring it out upon others. But the highest and most intimate state in this degree consists in a very simple and intimate exchange between God and the soul. The soul contemplates God constantly and is, so to speak, imperceptibly absorbed in what it sees and feels.

Often it sees quite well that it contemplates its divine Object in and by himself with a steady constancy, and its spirit is thus secretly satisfied. As long as the soul remains faithful to its introversion and maintains a very simple attention, it will continue to be satisfied.

All that we might still say on this subject would be far from the reality. Therefore, we must pass over it in silence, since it is the effect of the divine splendors, and takes place in a most secret silence, wherein God and all that is in him and of him is contemplated. Indeed, this most pure and continual contemplation, and simple enjoyment belong to anticipated glory, and are received in the deepest substance of the soul. They are bestowed upon the soul after it has been totally dissolved and consumed in the ardent and devouring fire of the Divinity, which penetrates its inmost substance.

(*Instructions for persevering in the state of transforming union*) In keeping with a very simple and naked gaze, the soul must maintain great attention in contemplating its divine Object. It should faithfully follow the simple, active and joyful inclination which draws it into the uncreated abyss of its infinite Object. But we should rather say that he who sometimes draws it, also keeps it immoveably fixed in himself, so that it may contemplate him. Here the soul is lost in his Totality beyond all distinction and difference. And if any distinction remains within the soul it is no longer evident, nor is it distinguishable even from the action of God within it. Hence, it must never alter its interior state for any reason whatsoever.

Here the soul must live a hidden life in purity and ignorance, as it keeps nature from subtly attaching itself to the images that spring up from the natural desire to know and to feel. This however, no longer occurs in the soul's present stage as it used to in the beginning, or in its advanced (*stage*). Now it is quite different and happens in an infinitely more subtle manner. Here the soul is strong and well established, and has control over its subtle inclinations. It is able to check the hidden activity of its faculties very simply. However, it must be attentive and constant, and carefully avoid all multiplicity. If it is to remain firmly settled in its delight and contemplation, it must die constantly to self.

Because they are in complete destitution, these souls find the listlessness of their faculties very painful—a common experience for those in this state. The remedy in this case is to keep the faculties free and active by one's own deliberate effort. The soul should simply and skillfully divert them from all curious and imaginary objects that are pleasant to nature, and as much as possible, keep them detached from created things. But since the sluggishness of the body often contributes to this listlessness, the soul must remedy it, if need be, by frequently changing posture.

Such a person should also carefully avoid disturbing the soul in its peace and suspension by seeking excessive and indiscreet bodily sufferings. When they come from God without its seeking them, then it must glory in them and esteem them. But if, through indiscretion, the soul is distracted by bodily sufferings and is invaded by all kinds of images, even though they are simple and spiritual, it will not enjoy the kind of spiritual repose that belongs to this state. Such action prevents the soul from following the very simple and unique attraction of God, Who fixes the soul in himself in an imperceptible manner. Ordinarily, it is quite imperceptible.

Elsewhere, I have spoken of the surrounding and pressing darkness of God, by which he draws certain souls into a more or less great oppression and anguish. He binds the faculties and keeps them in suspension, even to the point where he sometimes takes away the ability to reflect. However, he does not take away the ability to perform external actions that are commanded. The divine darkness is the Divinity, which thus makes itself obscure to the soul, and especially to the understanding. This faculty is surrounded by it and dazzled by the abundance of its blinding light. There, it is divinely elevated and suspended in admiration at the ravishing beauty of the Object which fills it. The soul is transported with the greatest delight as it contemplates the divine Object in a superessential manner, that is, in a completely naked, abstract and simple manner, in the superessential unity of God. Quite often it is elevated to this state without knowing what it is or where it is. God causes this darkness for his own greater glory and for the soul's perfection.

I must say, if these souls are elevated to this state while they are still imperfect and do not possess the virtues as acquired habits, I consider them lost. This certainly is not God's intention. It is the fault of the individual. And the reason for it I have already given elsewhere (Cf. Ch. 1 *Prayer*, p. 65). Suffice it to say that this state is in no way suited for them, because of their interior confusion and imperfection. Still, there can be no doubt that, if they so wished, it would not lead to their ruin, as it does for many. Besides, among such persons, his Majesty has pity on whom he pleases in order to preserve them from eternal death. Such loss follows only as a result of their spiritual sins which are blindness, pride, haste and similar miseries.

But the soul that is well tried, has acquired the virtues as habits and died to self, and most of all has attained to savorous contemplation and union of love, is not hurt by this divine darkness. Since it is humble and dead, and strengthened by the divine Spirit, it is disposed to bear this condition with wisdom and discretion. Still, it does not trust in its own wisdom and therefore, for safe guidance, communicates all its feelings to a director whom it knows to be accomplished in all such theory and practice.

1. Cf. glossary.
2. Cf. glossary.
3. Cf. glossary.
4. Cf. glossary.
5. Cf. glossary.
6. Cf. glossary.

CHAPTER IV

LOVE OF GOD

(*Obligation to love God*)   O man, love him who has loved you from
all eternity. Love him in all your actions and with all your powers.
To do less is not to love. Show your love through a worthy and
frequent reception of Holy Communion. Do not believe that your
state as a Christian or a religious can make you blessed. God's
love demands a return of love. Without a pure (*unselfish*) love,
exalted and singular spiritual practices only serve to inflate. Charity
alone edifies. On the other hand, we must avoid lukewarmness. It is
impossible to tell how much misery and spiritual poverty it brings
to those who live in-between, neither for God nor for themselves.
They have turned away from God to created things. Ordinarily,
they are unstable people, proud and filled with hypocrisy. They
show quite clearly that they have only themselves for their final
end and their instability for repose.

O my Beloved, may they learn to stir up an ardent enthusiasm
in themselves under the inspiring influence of your love. Then they
will become generous lovers. They will see how love thinks only of
the loved one, and is never idle, but proves itself in the joyful performance of good works. They will also see that love never grows
weary, and is not subject to reason. Shame does not restrain it,
and labor does not overcome it. It always begins anew without
looking back to the labor of the past. It sees only what remains
to be done and believes it is infinite. Still it is not frightened by
such a prospect. On the contrary, that fortifies it in a marvelous
and secret manner, and inspires it to turn frequently to you, its
sovereign happiness.

(*Value of love as a motive in our virtues and actions*)   Love may be present in all spiritual practices, but in the beginning it is not present in them as their motivating force. After the soul has acquired the habit of using love as the motive for its actions, it will be inclined to do and endure all things or leave them for love of God alone.

We must love our divine Spouse with a pure and ardent love, and by a constant practice of all the virtues. Let us never look upon any action or event as coming from creatures, but from the pure and most generous hand of God. He arranges the whole course of our life with wisdom, and leads us by ways that are not only pleasing to him but are also very conducive to our good. His providence is such a wonderful manifestation of his infinite goodness, that we are compelled to accept all things without question. Hence, we believe that love, which looks immediately to God as its end, should be the inspiring motive of all the virtues as the occasion for them arises.

It is not so much the performance of many works that you require of your elect, as an ardent and simple love, love that abhors any dissimilarity with your life more than death itself. Hence, all the glory of your spouses is within, in variety and diversity of virtues. There they dwell in solid seclusion, contemplating you in your infinite beauty. Wherever they turn, they see only evidences of your ecstatic love, which arouse profound admiration and inspire them anew to send forth new flames of love. As a result, they are raised higher and higher above themselves and all creatures in profound contemplation of you in your infinite and eternal abyss. Such is their life, conformed to you their model.

He who does not love you my Beloved, will never have either peace or rest, for there is no peace or rest except in you. Outside of you all is only vanity and affliction of spirit. As for the rest of the wicked, if they have it, we cannot call it a rest. It is the repose of an animal and even less than that. For animals always find what they desire according to their instinct because they were created thus.

(*Moderation to be exercised in sensible consolations*)   If the soul is

often filled to overflowing with love and light, even in its sense
faculties, the body becomes weakened and enfeebled by such favors.
Hence, when it is under the influence of such sensible consolations,
it must not pay too much attention to them, nor should it follow
their attraction. It should then look for holy, external occupations,
such as reading, studying, praying and similar tasks, if they can
be found. After these sensible impressions have passed, the soul
should once more resume its gentle and unique introversion,[1] as well
as its simple, unitive love.

While it should ordinarily pay no attention to such impressions,
it should however, concentrate on those that are sound. For they
are simple and dilate the soul with light. Nor do they become
coarse by overflowing into the body or the inferior part (*of the
soul*). The first attractions are not bad, providing the soul follows
the advice we have given above. But the latter are pure and more
worthy of the divine Spouse. And they are more suited for souls
who are already eminently and perfectly reformed. Under their
influence they feel the Spouse entering more gently, simply and
abundantly into the inmost depth of their spirit, depending on the
degree of their transformation. This advice is of the greatest
importance.

(*True love and false love*)   True love has five stages. The first is that
of infancy, the stage wholly given to milk. The second begins after
separation from the breast. The third is that of adolescence. The
fourth is the stage of maturity. The fifth is that of perfect man-
hood. During these stages, souls, who are sincerely in love with
God, have their ups and downs. There are periods of joy and sadness,
of light and darkness. There are times of prosperity and adversity,
of riches and poverty, of delights and languors. The soul experiences
seasons of peace and war, of strength and weakness, moments when
it has everything, and then, nothing. If they remain faithful, they
will suffer no harm, because, for sincere lovers, all things work
unto good.

Such vicissitudes, so varied and often crucifying, are meant to
test souls to see whether they serve their Spouse for unselfish
reasons, or merely as hirelings, seeking only his gifts. If they serve

as hirelings, when these gifts fail them, their love for their Spouse also fails. Thus we see that they do not love him in and for himself, but only in and for themselves. It is a matter for great regret, because they persist in worshipping the wonderful gifts of God as idols, selfishly keeping them for themselves, and using them according to their own wishes. It is quite evident that they are full of self love. On the other hand, faithful souls do not serve or love God for their own particular interests. They remain firm and steadfast lovers of him in all the vicissitudes we have described above.

A great deal could be said about the feeling of love, for example, how natural it is to many who are by nature sentimental, and how difficult it is to distinguish between divine love and natural love. No matter what our intention may be, I do not think that our love is entirely holy, pure and unselfish, in view of the fact that in things which we desire very much, it is very difficult for our nature to avoid seeking its own pleasure. In things that are delightful to the concupiscible appetite, this selfishness works so subtly that we are not even aware of it. But where there can be no question of pleasure or even of benefits that are so agreeable to our nature, there is little to fear. In such cases, we are quite indifferent about having or not having, doing or not doing, giving or retaining, knowing or not knowing, refusing or accepting. Then we can be quite sure that a good and simple intention is sufficient to purify our love and our work.

But when we have an ardent desire to do something, this ardor or natural activity is a clear sign that our motives and our actions are not pure. It is much safer not to follow our inclinations and attractions at once. And the holier they appear to be, the more must we beware of self, because our love for what is good ought to look at God alone. It should seek the most perfect union with him, the union of our all with the All of God.

Of this we can be very certain, where there is humility, mortification and self-contempt, there is no self-love. Nor is it present when there is question of dying (*to self*), or of accepting something that causes aversion or demands constant resignation. Two contraries cannot exist together, such as living and dying, living according to self-love and dying (*to it*). Self-love must die and be completely destroyed if the love of God is to rule the soul as its own kingdom.

Now I have revealed some profound secrets to you, secrets that are quite hidden and quite mystical. But some day, with God's help, you will understand them, after you have grown in love, knowledge and practical experience.

All this is so marvelous that it fills men with exultation, wonder and rejoicing. Such is God's game with his poor and miserable servants. Because they have served him faithfully, they are allowed to share his infinite love in an extraordinary manner. So do your best and practice these things continually, but maintain a habit of indifference. Place all your joy and delight in serving only his Majesty. Live completely for this, as though God and yourself were the only ones in this world.

The true lover, who remains steadfast in his abandonment, is much stronger than he thinks. Often when he thinks he is lying on the ground, he is actually on his feet, and has won a complete victory over self, over nature and even over the devils. O God, how wretched we are when left all alone! But how strong and how rich we are, when we are surrounded on all sides by our Beloved, even though we are not aware of it. Such is the hidden method used by God to preserve us in our purity and in our riches. He withdraws himself and his gifts from our sight, and sometimes even seems to withdraw faith, hope and charity.

In these grievous languors the just soul lives by faith, and adheres to God in a simple and naked manner by means of a pure and simple charity. In this state it chooses the bitter chalice and the painful cross with its great torments, so as to remain firmly fixed in God, in preference to all the precious gifts that he could ever give it. And even if it is tried by the most evil and insistent temptations, it is only distressed externally, because it posesses a divine peace within.

We have been created in order to return to God through love, through his own love. In us it must be ardent, pure and unceasingly active, so that we expend all our energies and are consumed by it. Actually, we shall never be able to do or give anything that can sufficiently recompense him who is infinite Love. Before him every creature is deceitful, and in comparison with him, man is nothing.

My Beloved, you command me to love you. Even if I had not received such a command, I would still love you, because of what you are. For you are infinitely worthy of my love, aside from the external manifestation of your love for men and angels, and especially for me, the most miserable of sinners. Therefore, it is not exalted feelings I desire, but to love you in truth. And although I am certain there will be a great deal of work to do when I begin to attack my enemies, I am also certain that you will make it your concern to clothe me with yourself and with your gifts. Once my faculties and my desires have been reformed, all will become perfect according to the degree foreseen and ordained by you from all eternity. This I hope to attain through your love and infinite mercy.

Indeed, my Beloved, the same Goodness and Mercy that brought about your Incarnation daily reforms those who desire you. I too await this blessing with patience and humility, and my trust in you will never fail even though I receive it later than I wish. In the meantime, I will do what little I can. And, in all events, I will seek repose in you through resignation and constant conformity to your will. What reason for anxiety can he have to whom you owe nothing? Therefore, since I have received so many graces from you and don't know where to begin describing even a part of them, I ought to return to you with a pure, deep and grateful love, ready to give up my life a thousand times as an odor of sacrifice.

Hence, my Beloved, I am deeply obliged to anchor myself in you, in your love and infinite goodness. I shall therefore create esteem for them through my misery, misery which you have entirely reformed, thus enabling me to live in you and for you alone. I do not expect you to accomplish these things in me by a sensible love, or in some manner accomodated to my wishes. Do it, my Life, at such a time and in such a manner as will please you. It is for you to guide me and try me in the ways of your love. And it is for me to sustain you lovingly and humbly, without ever wavering in the faith and fidelity I owe you.

If it were possible to enjoy the happiness and glory of the

blessed without loving you, I would not want it. But that cannot
be so, since the complete happiness of the blessed consists not
so much in seeing you as in loving you, loving you not only as
God, but also as God-Man, and Savior of men, the source of happiness for our bodies and our souls, for our whole being. For if the
blessed were blessed only in seeing you, and not in loving you,
then you would be all beauty, but not all goodness. Thus they
would be happy only in themselves. That would make their beati-
tude as imperfect as it is actually perfect in loving you with a
supreme love. Therefore, to see you and to love you constitute
one and the same happiness.

Love, if it is genuine, is found in everything, in poverty and
in abundance. In the many vicissitudes of nature, it never changes
or turns away from its Object, whether it be in torments, in death,
in life, or in anything whatever. If this were not the case, my Love,
you would not have such a great number of saints enjoying infinite
goodness in varying degrees of sanctity.

As for me, O my Beloved, you have never been indebted to me
for anything, and yet you have always given me all that was
in you in each of your actions. It is a thing worthy of eternal
admiration, considering what you are and what I am. All that is
yours and mine, you have acquired in the poor and painful state
of my nature. And if I do not always imitate you perfectly through
love and the practice of all the virtues, who will repay my debts
to you? Even if I were able to sacrifice myself for you a thousand
times, it would never repay my debt. Therefore, what can I do,
except to do my best to surrender to you, for I see all the earth
filled with your prodigies like an infinite sea!

It is quite true to say that no one becomes perfect suddenly.
Time, method and practice are necessary to arrive at love. Hence,
we cannot sufficiently deplore the misery of the man who, instead
of using the gifts you have bestowed upon him in order to know
and love you as his sovereign Good, uses them only for himself,
in order to know the visible things outside of him, or in him. Now
the more you see that your spouses delight in you, the more you
communicate yourself through the most delightful exercises. And
the more you bless and enrich them with your favors and caresses,

the more pleasure and delight they take in returning to you. They seek only you, in spite of the abundant gifts you bestow on them. For themselves they desire only constant contempt and confusion. They suffer much over their dissimilarities with you, whether past or present, but in simplicity. For it is your love that permits this difference so that they may feel their faults like a painful burden.

(*Degrees of love and their effects*)   For his own glory and for the good and humiliation of those who serve him, God often permits souls, in the beginning of their conversion, to perform acts of virtue with ease. For this reason, he even floods them with great sweetness without them being any the more perfect for it, inasmuch as they have not yet acquired real mortification. This is why beginners advance towards God quite differently. Some draw near to him quite quickly, while the generality remain crawling on the ground. Certain ones advance by gradual stages to the door of sovereign good. But the favorites are introduced into it, as it were, all of a sudden. There, for a certain time, they remain in loving adoration at the feet of Jesus. Then, by rising to a higher degree of love they dwell in adoration at his divine hands. Finally, by a subtle elevation, they arrive at His most sacred mouth, which they adore and kiss a thousand times on each occasion. All these souls discover streams, fountains and rivers of love which produce all kinds of delightful affections, all diversely suited to each one's state.

Just as the sun has diverse effects on the earth according as it is near or far from it, thus making it fruitful for the good of mankind, so does the divine Son of Justice produce diverse effects of his love in men; in some quite soon, in others after some time, all in different degrees, according as he finds the earth of their hearts disposed for them by grace. Out of love God wishes to enrich souls with his grace in an ever greater degree. He adorns them with his beauty and living splendors in order to make them perfect lovers.

Thus, under the influence of the divine favors, these souls strip off the old man and put on the new man who is divine. Depending on the degree of grace they have received, divine Wisdom produces a great variety of wonders in the spiritual earth of their souls. In those who are learning to die to self God produces these wonders through frequent ups and downs, and through the marvelous effects of his love. As they respond to the attractions of divine love they become so absorbed in it that they live only by love and for love.

Now God gives his love to whom he pleases, and for this reason gradually lifts man up to himself, so that he may love beyond all reason. And because he is full of love, he accomplishes and endures great things without growing weary. In the beginning this love is sensible and easy, but when it is perfect, and even when it is only in the advanced stage, it is very naked and simple, and beyond all understanding.

The love that belongs to ordinary charity is only reasonable, and does not go beyond reason. Its acts are, so to speak, done by constraint. And if it reaches the point of suffering, it only becomes an act of patience supported by reason. For if, at times, it performs some actions that are more noble and generous, we are still very doubtful as to whether they come from nature or grace.

If, what a person must do or suffer is very contrary to his desire and beyond natural reason, then it is undoubtedly the result of grace. However, when he does something good for someone without being actually motivated by love and the will of God, he is ordinarily acting only according to the instinct of pure nature. For nature performs a kindness in order to receive a similar one in return. Such a motive is enough to make it perform or endure great things. It may also be able to do this through strength of character.

But the love that springs from a charity that is active and unselfish is constantly at work, both on occasions that require suffering as well as action. While it is reasonable, it never grows weary nor is it overcome. Such love is always faithful, whether it be in the senses, or above sense and reason. I must point out that, although sensible love reasons in order to love, it does not therefore lose its excellence, for it comes from God. But I must also admit that sensible love, no matter how elevated is not as noble or as excellent as the love that is detached, simple and totally withdrawn from the senses. Such love enables the soul to endure all things as if they were outside of it and at its own cost.

Ordinary charity is concerned with externals, and seems to be nothing else than a rectitude of natural reason. It is vanquished by the faults of others. And the great external works of those who live only in this stage, are as it were, only mud and earth. On the other hand, real love demands that the soul be simple and uniform, not divided or multiplied by the works of the active life. But those who live only in the active life look to it for their satisfaction, thinking they will merit a great deal by it. Consequently they look for more and more work in it.

But a life that is truly interior draws a person inward to unity of heart by a simple and loving inclination. Inspired by an incessant love which influences all its faculties, the soul desires to imitate Jesus Christ more according to his divinity than according to his humanity. Actually, this second form of imitation always follows the first one. The soul looks very lovingly at this God clothed in our human flesh. In his infinite love he united himself so closely and perfectly to it that he is one and the same Person in two natures, divine and human, God and Man. Thus his life, his actions and sufferings are divine. This sight of the God-Man ravishes the soul with a most profound wonder, and absorbs it in a sea of infinite abysses and secret mysteries. It sees how the immense love of his Heart embraces heaven and earth, and is capable of consuming infinitely more without suffering any diminution.

This profound impression transports the soul into the immense fire of his love where it is melted, and entirely consumed. Its only desire is to live there in imitation of its beloved Object. It accomplishes this by observing a number of simple, loving and essential practices. Thus it grieves for its beloved Object, and feels compassion for him. It admires him and sighs for him. When contemplating him, it often sends forth keen darts of its deepest love toward him. At such times it annihilates, humbles and dilates itself depending on the attractions, splendors and other divine effects which God produces in it. To all of these divine favors the soul gives a wholehearted and unreserved response. God raises it up to himself from light to light, until it has accomplished the work of total transformation, and has reached the highest peak of perfection. Thus, in a short time, its intention and affection become perfect, while its love grows correspondingly simple.

This exalted way of love is a very short path to the enjoyment of every blessing. To practice it the soul has no need of theory. Nor is it necessary to devote itself completely to external things, or to the consideration of created things. All that is contrary to this path, and the less time the soul gives to it, the more it is suited to enter the way of love. Nevertheless, a good character is an excellent disposition for arriving there. But those, who lie on the outside and want to rest there in the active life, will never have the kind of intention that does all for God alone. Nor will they ever arrive at the glories and delights of the interior life.

Moreover, the soul that has reached this stage of simplicity avoids what would entangle it exteriorly or interiorly. It places infinitely more value on being simple in its inmost being, to which it is completely reduced, than upon all that its own faculties might be able to produce in order to keep it interiorly and exteriorly occupied. If for the moment it has some attractive interior occupation, it is God who provides it for reasons best known to him and as it pleases him. Meanwhile the soul remains fixed in this state in order to look steadily and simply upon its Object. There it seeks its repose and happiness. Since there are no forms or images in this state, the soul is very careful not to dwell upon them, no matter how subtly. Moreover, since God is seen and relished here, and actually possessed in himself by a naked and simple look, the soul should desire nothing else. Its spirit is now completely transfused.

Being deeply recollected, the soul carefully avoids being drawn away from this state, especially when the senses put pressure upon it, seeking relief. They urge it very subtly to occupy itself with the most exalted objects. Actually the senses are seeking their own secret satisfaction for they always want to see and feel something new. But the faithful and prudent soul patiently endures these subtle impressions without injury, and without contributing anything to them. On the contrary this experience makes it seek greater recollection. It has an even greater determination to look at its Object who draws it into himself and ravishes it out of the senses and out of itself. There it enjoys its delights in a simple and ineffable manner. Hence it ignores these distractions even to the point of forgetting itself.

In order not to stray from this state, such a soul must carefully avoid subtly seeking itself by turning the death of the senses into an obsession. It ought to live entirely lost to itself without reflecting upon its exalted position, and only for the pleasure of him whom it desires to please in this perpetual and profound death. Although this kind of life requires a simple and naked faith, it is permissible sometimes to speak to God in vocal and affectionate converse. This is done, not for the purpose of introverting oneself, but simply because it is appropriate, because love that is perfectly consummated often requires it as an act of benevolence. From this we can see that the soul ought to develop a hidden strength in order to remain firmly established in the constant contemplation and fruition of its Object, no matter what happens. For the highest state of this divine strength—it is the last one, because of its simple and profound eminence—enables the soul to be patient in its continual deaths. On this matter there is nothing more we can say. Indeed, once the soul has arrived at this state, it no longer endures any other death, except the deaths of being helpless. This is a very profound secret.

(*Pure love is not founded on reason*) When reason is needed in order to love, (*pure*) love is not present, inasmuch as love is able by itself to draw and ravish one's whole being in unity of spirit without the help of studied reasons. Moreover, lovers who are experienced in the science of love, prefer to die a thousand deaths, so to speak, rather than bolster their *active* and *passive* love with purely reasonable motives. They prefer to be pierced by a thousand arrows rather than seek consolation and support in the senses and in created things. They no longer wish to depend on them, because they see that the way of reason is infinitely distant from the unique and efficacious way of sincere and pure love. Therefore, in order to direct their unique and objective love to God alone, they constantly make ardent, simple and brief aspirations.

Indeed, the faithful practice of aspiration by a soul that is deeply wounded with love is one of the holiest that the Saints can exercise in this life. For, when it is exercised in action, it is based upon pure and simple love, and when it endures suffering, it is based upon pure and naked love. When it is faithful in love, the soul abandons itself to grievous afflictions and languors which its Well-Beloved makes it suffer in his presence, but without showing himself to it. Hence, it endures a sorrowful desolation and grievous languor, during which it dies, because of its impatient but tranquil love, in the arms of its Spouse. Still it has no desire to use the senses or created things in order to look for him either inside or outside.

All this is easy to say, but hard to do. It is difficult to endure, and very difficult to surmount. For the soul must remain firm and immovable, and constantly preserve a simple repose that is above action and intention, and above the present sensible manifestation of the Spouse. It does this because it believes that it cannot do otherwise, and because it feels that the Beloved should never be obliged to return again in order to bestow the kiss of his mouth upon his chaste spouse.

Here human endeavor is useless. The active interchange between the Spouse and his beloved now ceases—a perfect test of its fidelity. For the generous and constant endurance of the Beloved's absence causes extreme suffering, especially when the soul refuses to look for consolation either outside or inside, directly or indirectly. It consoles itself only with its desolation, its plaints and loving laments. In them, if it still has any strength, it speaks to its Spouse of its sorrowful and anguished regrets. Otherwise, it complains even more sorrowfully in the midst of its complete suspension, its painful agonies and languor, by means of a continual glance directed toward its Spouse.

Thus, the loving soul suffers more than words can express. Still without being aware of it, it keeps an attentive gaze fixed upon its Spouse, even though the activity of its faculties is completely suspended. For, although it has often experienced the rigors of its Spouse's absence in the preceding stages, this stage is much more painful to it. Here it seems to be very inexperienced in suffering, because of the severe effects, which are quite different from its previous experiences. It doesn't know, so to speak, whether it is dead or alive; whether it belongs to itself or to its Spouse. Its sole consolation is that no creature can console it for the loss which it thinks it has incurred. Actually, it is still in possession of its Well-Beloved, but without knowing it or believing it, not however, without ardently and eagerly desiring him. That alone is evidence that it truly possesses him who draws and ravishes the highest part of the soul to himself. Indeed, the soul dwells and exists completely in him, although deprived of his sensible and luminous consolations. There, in secret solitude, it gazes upon him while it laments its supposed misfortune.

The soul must therefore fortify itself with patience and constancy, so as never to veer either to right or to left, doing nothing else but suffer, and waiting with full and loving confidence for the blessed and happy return of its Spouse. Completely stripped of self and of every satisfaction, it must be resigned and detached, conforming itself completely to the divine will and ready to suffer the rigors of this winter for time and eternity. By this I mean the absence of its Spouse, the feeling of being deprived of him and of being completely dull in its feelings.

It is very important for those who wish to love, to realize that sanctity and fidelity in love do not consist in having great thoughts, revelations, visions, sensible visits and outpourings of God, but in giving God pleasure without seeking their own satisfaction. Furthermore, it consists in suffering and in patiently enduring the withdrawal of the Beloved. This is intended to prevent souls from indulging in a gluttonous desire to possess God more for their own sake than for his sake. Therefore, let them give him pleasure by lamenting in every possible manner, but especially by their patience and simple resignation. With these dispositions, they deliver themselves as victims to him together with all their actions, in a state of conformity and deiformity. To act in this manner all one's life is to be in the world, but not of it.

From this we see that souls in this degree of pure love ought to be fervent and interiorly busy, so as to be idle as little as possible.

They ought to open up and spend themselves in returning the *pure* love of their Spouse, employing all their strength in this work, until they are completely consumed in the fire of divine love which will transform them into itself.

I have described this state in its perfection after it has been acquired by a soul that is loving and faithful. Now I must explain it in its principles and beginnings. He who practices them will be able to acquire it in its highest perfection, just as we described it above.

Those who are capable of loving and have made some progress in the spiritual life should resolve to love God constantly and fervently during prayer and outside of it by the practice of simple aspirations. Although they are composed of only a few words, they lift the soul up entirely into God, and do not permit any sensible division between the two (i.e., *God and the soul*). Once it has experienced these effects in the way advanced souls do, it will be quite convinced that aspiration is an effective means to acquire the highest perfection. In its practice let it use only the best motive, namely, pure love. Such love does not need reasons to be convinced into loving its divine Object.

With this same motive it is very easy to practice all the virtues when the occasion demands it. For one, who has flown the heights, can easily descend to a lower plane. Therefore, it ought to be very easy for the faithful lover to accept contempt and self-annihilation when occasions present themselves, either because of his faults and miseries, or because of his neighbor. Certainly, he ought to be very happy to have such opportunities for humiliation in order to see himself as he is.

Since all the virtues come from a genuine humility, or better, from a perfectly humble love, we reduce all the virtues to love. For the virtues should never be separated from love, except in their actual practice. But in their essence they ought to be united in the essence of love. Such is the simple means used by the soul when it is active in the practice of simple, interior love. Note that it must act in the strength and perfection of pure love as a motive both in its exterior and interior practices, without making any distinction between them. Just as God expresses his fruitfulness externally by a single, perpetual act in accordance with its eternal purpose, so must we undertake the performance of distracting things as willingly and as easily as we embrace those that are interior. And although these external works may be mean and distracting, still, they are presented to us by God, not by men. Hence, we must abandon ourselves completely to him and remain firmly fixed in the inmost depth of our spirit, where we maintain a constant union with the Object of our love by means of a simple gaze. This gaze will be above the simple intention. There is no need to describe minutely the various external works to which the soul will be drawn. Suffice it to say that in this state we must be resolved to let ourselves be inspired and moved by God as much as he wishes, and in whatever way he wishes. Actual love is the cause of love, and increases it to the highest possible degree. But those, who have not yet attained perfect love, must work strictly on the virtues, and that out of love for God. They should persevere until they have acquired them as habits, and have such a strong desire for them that they can practice the virtues on every occasion. Therefore, I advise souls in the state of pure love to be as active as possible, and eagerly invent affectionate ways of conversing and uniting themselves with God. Such behavior makes the soul extremely expert in forming simple and familiar aspirations. At the same time it enables the soul always to avoid the slightest differences with God in its desires, words and actions.

Although love is the same in essence, it has many names and degrees due to its various effects in the soul and the stages through which it must pass in order to reach its inaccessible Origin. One of the principal degrees is intense and profound love, the practice of which brings the soul to the more sublime stages. Once it has attained these stages through the many labors of love and the complete consummation of self, the soul finds rest. As it advances in the spiritual life under the sensible and hidden influences of God, the work of love becomes simple and easy. Moreover, God works in us according to the quality of our spiritual exercises. If they are lively, ardent and continual, he communicates himself to us in a similar manner, until his divine influence is so frequent and abundant that we find ourselves completely adorned with all the virtues and the seven gifts of the Holy Spirit without, as it were, being aware of it.

The method for practicing this ardent love is short and easy. Its subject is constant and loving aspiration. But to be perfect, aspiration must be practiced so eagerly and continually that it becomes as easy as breathing. It has a number of degrees, all of which can be reduced to four. The *first* consists in offering oneself and all created things to God. As far as possible, this should be done in an abstract manner (i.e., *spiritually or detached from sense feelings*). The *second* degree consists in making requests of the divine Spouse, asking him for his gifts in him and for his own sake. The *third* degree consists in being resigned and completely conformed to him. This conformity is very lofty and perfect, and is characterized by great love. Moreover, the soul also desires it for creatures who are capable of such exalted love. The *fourth* degree is that of unitive love which unites the soul to God. Here the soul yearns for him and pursues him with acts of love until he opens his loving and superessential bosom to it. Here it feasts upon his immense beauty in great abundance and intoxication, eating and drinking at the table of the Blessed. But since this does not last very long the soul soon returns to itself to feed upon its former spiritual fare. From this it derives renewed strength, until God again receives it into his bosom with the same effect. This degree is very exalted and contains the preceeding degrees in their most perfect form. However, the first three degrees may also be practiced with a profound and perfect union besides the last one. This depends on the soul's progress in aspiration. But in the last degree, the soul's only occupation, by which it seeks its Well-Beloved, is that of union itself.

These four degrees are the principal means used by the soul to express its love for its Spouse. Through the zealous practice of them, it will attain an ever greater perfection in God. It will then go from one abyss of profound delight to another, until it reaches the ultimate abyss—infinite in depth—where the soul will be wholly lost in God and swallowed up with exceeding joy in its eternal Origin.

When the soul has constantly and ardently practiced aspirative love according to the four degrees mentioned above, it receives loving caresses from God in greater or lesser number according to its progress. At the same time it receives such ardent and efficacious outpourings of love that the continual enjoyment of its Beloved produces an ever more ardent desire for him. Finding itself so intimately embraced by him, the soul is at a complete loss as to how to respond to this overflowing torrent of his love which keeps it dilated in the river of divine delights. In this state of simple and delightful intoxication, the ardent desire and joyful inclination of the soul are increasingly sharpened and excited by the loving embraces of its Spouse. And when it sees all its efforts reduced to nothing by the fire of the divine understanding, it succumbs before the splendor of his ravishing beauty.

But this state does not last very long, for God soon withdraws himself (i.e., *his sensible and delightful influence*) from his kingdom. The soul is now obliged to knock anew at the door, and to continue this sweet and loving action until it is once more received into the bosom of its most beloved and chaste Spouse. The ensuing state is far more pleasant for the soul than the preceeding one. As these comings of the Spouse succeed each other they give greater depth to the soul and draw it to greater simplification. At the same time its capacity for enjoying divine delights also grows, for the soul experiences them in the very essence of God, in whom it is totally transformed. In this divine action the powers of the whole man receive a growing splendor and adornment with each experience of these profound touches. And it is all done for the sole pleasure of the Spouse.

Completely intoxicated with delight and, as it were, infatuated with love for its Beloved, the soul cries out amid the affluence of its delights, "My Well-Beloved is mine; he will abide between my breasts," that is, he will possess its heart and soul forever, no matter what the cost, even though it be a thousand lives. God delights it with an entirely new communication of himself, and floods it with his luminous and delicious gifts—abundant graces which he has never before given to the soul.

Out of this experience, active on one side and passive on the

other, arises the vivifying life. It banishes all desire for and remembrance of the dying life and even of the purely reasonable life.

The transformation of the soul and the intimate possession of it
by God is accomplished by the exalted practice of aspiration, or,
by simple and essential inclinations. These inclinations contain in
their highest perfection, all that is comprised in vocal and prolonged aspiration. They are very simple and lofty glances of the
soul which touch and inflame the highest point of the will with
simple love for its Spouse. This love is above the understanding
and all that is sensible.

In this degree of transformation the soul says to its Spouse,
"You are what I am, and I am what you are without there being
any difference between us." Continuing in this spirit of admiration,
it says to him, "You are beautiful my Well-Beloved," and the
Spouse replies in turn, "You are beautiful my beloved, my dove,
my love and delight. Your beauty comes from me and is in me.
I have desired it," because you went in search of me with a
yearning love. In the most secret chamber of your heart you came
lovingly to see me and to hear me alone speak. This should convince you of the fact that I have known and desired your beauty
in order to enter into a solemn and eternal marriage with you,
and to transform you into what I am for myself. Thus you see
that I am truth itself. In my greatness you see your littleness.
In my all, your nothingness, which is finally absorbed by it. Therefore, let us consummate our mutual love in the bond of the most
Holy Spirit, and in inaccessible unity above all understanding.
Let us enjoy each other to the fullest in mutual delights. For
this reason I will come and visit you continually, renewing our
love and our joy in the consummation of this mutual enjoyment.
My spouse and my most beloved, I no longer wish you to say,
"Let him kiss me with the kiss of his mouth." I want to embrace
you very lovingly, with your mouth fixed to mine, so that you
may delight in my pleasant and ardent sighing, and I in yours.
Such will be the mutual delight of two lovers who have become one
single spirit in the sweet and ardent strength of him who is the

most exalted of the two. I, the eternal source of all happiness and the perfection of my chaste spouses, will bring about the perfect conversion, and total transformation of this soul.

In this state of intimate and profound enjoyment, the soul does not know what to do or to think in response to the love which floods its whole being. Obviously it is very difficult for it to restrain itself and avoid manifesting something of its interior rapture by signs and unusual gestures. Just as sweet wine when placed in a cask under force often overflows its container by its impetuosity, so this love quite often refuses to remain confined within the limited capacity of the interior faculties without manifesting itself by certain external signs. At such a time, the soul is under the impression that everyone experiences this love together with its accompanying wisdom and delights. It has forgotten the meaning of sorrow and affliction, and thinks that its profound peace and joy, and the sweetness and simplicity of its interior life will last forever. Still, when it becomes fearful of some approaching trial, it fortifies itself with the most fervent desires, and thus remains firm and impregnable when it encounters contradiction and desolation.

Indeed, the soul feels no repugnance to this at all within its faculties, because they are sensibly possessed by God, filled with him and with divine sentiments. Or they may be so filled with his superabundance that it overflows into all their faculties, causing great dilation. Hence, under the influence of this active and mutual love the soul lives in a paradise of delights, as far removed from the created objects surrounding it, as if they did not even exist. For, although it performs external actions for its own needs or those of its neighbor either out of obedience or charity, its attention is fixed only upon the beatific Object which draws and ravishes it above itself, and often out of itself. It does this by means of certain simple, impetuous transports which are so strong and sweet that they at once carry away the soul and all its faculties to joyful union with the Beloved. In this union it sees and understands the height, depth, breadth and length of God himself who holds it in his embrace, and seems to desire its complete annihilation. All this is accomplished in the soul with a knowledge and delight that defy description, notwithstanding the soul's previous experiences.

But alas! Since the divine Spouse desires nothing so much as the perfection of his beloved, even to its complete consummation in the fullness of his love, he often leaves it quite suddenly, when it least expects it. For example, he will do this while it is sleeping profoundly in his delightful bosom.

Therefore, when he suddenly deprives it of his luminous and delightful presence, the spouse suddenly awakens to find that it has gone from one extreme to the other. Now it no longer sees or feels anything but itself. Quite often it is very confused and suffers persistent attacks from the senses, the flesh and the devils, to whom the Spouse has given liberty in these painful trials. However, he does this only for the soul's greater perfection, thereby showing that it is as dear and pleasing to him as ever. For his Majesty is determined to sanctify and transform it in the fullness of his own likeness so that he may be able to say to it 'You are all beautiful my beloved, my spouse. There is no spot or stain of self-love in you,' for now, you receive me and my gifts in me and for myself, and not for yourself.

Despite this fact, the soul is, to a certain extent, unaware of the exalted design of its Beloved, and doesn't know what to do or think of its grievous and lamentable state, and the painful absence of its Spouse. In its anguish the soul seeks to make good its loss by tears, sighs and laments uttered in the depths of its heart . . . . If its plaints are not manifested in this particular manner, then they are expressed with even greater distress by its patience, by ardent glances and by complete, essential and mute conversions of the soul toward its Beloved.

But finally, after so many sorrowful and touching aspirations, the Beloved, moved with compassion, returns suddenly in a momentary act, like a flash of lightning. In this encounter the soul feels completely renewed. Darkness vanishes and is succeeded by an infinite light. Its former multiplicity and distractions cease to exist and all is reduced to unity of spirit. Now it experiences a new attraction as it is transported and caressed by Jesus Christ, its Spouse and Lover. Profoundly dilated, it abides in his divinity in a state of complete liquefaction. All its anguished laments are completely forgotten, as if they had never existed.

In addition to the union already described, there are other degrees which may be attained by an intense, loving practice of our *Soliloquies* and aspirative exercises. For this, the soul will need a more ardent love, especially in the beginning of this state, rather than a great deal of learning and knowledge of God. In order to make progress in the transforming love of the divine essence, it is even necessary, so to speak, to be in complete ignorance. For exalted thoughts and theological speculations only stuff the intellect. Consequently there is an infinite distance between perfect and profound aspiration, and intellectual consideration even though the latter is occupied with the things of God and the interior life.

Rest assured, that, if you act thus (i.e., *imitate the virtues of Jesus*), and wish to lose yourself entirely, without attaching yourself to the gifts of God in you,—although you must not refuse them, but must draw from them the fruit that God wishes—you will soon attain the highest love of God. Under its dominion and powerful inspiration, you will find it as easy to practice this love as it is to breathe. The reason is, that since this love is infinite its activity, in keeping with its purpose, ought to be quite easy. But here it is not so much a question of an active love as of a passive love, a love given to complete renunciation at all times. Thus it is resigned to feel or not to feel the graces and gifts of God. This attitude is very good for us, because it enables us to give God more pleasure than in the preceeding state. For this reason, we must resolve, as far as possible, to leave nothing undone and to endure all things according to God's good pleasure.

Now this is a profound secret, namely, when love is practiced for itself by the whole subject in the whole of its Object in an eminent manner, it is far different in state and condition from the love that lives and acts only according to the will of God. When you are completely lost in the vast ocean of love, you will know that I am speaking the truth. I wanted very much to tell you this so that you would be encouraged to leave what is less perfect and aim at the highest perfection.

For those who are faithful in sustaining it, the practice of naked and essential love is an excellent method for knowing oneself and attaining deep humility. It has many degrees of perfection. But it is very difficult to endure. Only those who persevere in its practice can be really called faithful. As they faithfully and courageously bear the sorrows and agonies of this kind of love, their likeness to the Beloved becomes more perfect. However, I do not intend to discuss theory but practice. For I wish souls would be so faithful in the practice of love that they would merit to know the whole of the mystical life and its ways by experience rather than by instruction. When he finds souls perfectly disposed by his grace, God himself accomplishes it by a succession of abundant touches and attractions. As for the vivid descriptions given by human authors, they are mere stammerings compared to the reality.

Therefore, as long as a man fails to go beyond his own activity, he simply will not understand what we are talking about. He may be quite faithful to external practices, but, until he has gone beyond their ultimate purpose, which is to inflame his heart with such a desire to praise God that he doesn't know how to praise him sufficiently, he will not attain the interior practices. This desire belongs to what the mystics call a *constantly active love*. Now love has many other degrees of perfection, all of which come from interior practices, but this last effect is the entrance to it. So without any further hesitation, let the soul close its eyes and set out on this path.

(*Love destroys our faults. He is speaking of souls who energetically practice all the virtues, but still have faults of frailty. However, they do not remain in them for long, but rise up and, with even greater love, ardently plunge into God, their center of love.*)   Faults of frailty in such souls are very useful and fruitful not as faults, but insofar as the soul is inspired to destroy them by the practice of a vigorous love. Thus they lose nothing of their spiritual eminence. On the contrary, much to the pleasure of God, they increase it by a constant fidelity which makes them prefer to die a thousand times over rather than stagnate on the ground, that is, in the senses or in creatures, no matter how perfect they may be. Instead, they at once return to God with ardent love and lose themselves in his abundant and ineffable joy.

This thought should strengthen our love so that we may attain to God and remain in him as in our place of repose. There our soul will enjoy this infinitely happy Object with great love and delight according to the degree of its infused and acquired love. Thus it will be transformed into him in an ever greater degree, becoming like him in love, joy and light. It will become his all, not by nature but by grace and love.

Such are the good effects that spring from the faults of the children of love. But there is a great difference and a great distance between those who fall and those who get up. For, if love is genuine, the faults are never big ones and they are occasions for practicing profound humility, because true love is also genuinely humble. This, however, does not prevent the soul from enjoying a holy and well-ordered liberty of spirit. True, when love is strong, a soul quite often goes to spiritual excess, and persons of a much lesser flight and incapable of such love, are scandalized by it. Such external excesses are an indication that the *must* (or, *unfermented element*) of fervent love is not well directed. Hence, the soul is carried away by this most delightful spiritual inebriation, and the effects of it become evident in its actions. Thinking that all men burn with the same fire and are intoxicated with the same love that completely dominates it, it reveals its thoughts to others. Therefore, it is evident that these disorders, which render a man more patient, and transport him out of himself, do not make him blameworthy in the remotest possible way.

Since we are human and very imperfect pilgrims upon this earth, we should detest even the slightest venial sin. We never fall into them except through lack of fervor or through imprudence. Hence, of all the means for avoiding it, a fervent active love is the most necessary. And if we are sincerely faithful, our loving absorption will keep us far from such sins. For an active love blots out venial sins sooner and more effectively than a less fervent use of the Sacrament of Penance, because you take great pleasure in the practice of such love. Like little straws in a fire, such sins are instantly destroyed in the consuming fire of your love. Consequently, the more the soul is absorbed by love, the more it forgets its sins, even in confession. This is a fact that is very little known.

(*Trials of love: suffering. For advanced souls in time of aridity, he recommends the following practice:*) You must not make sorrowful and lamenting cries with too impetuous an effort. That is dangerous, and would produce even greater darkness in you. But you must gently send forth simple and essential glances toward God, sighing and yearning for his presence from the deepest depth of your soul. Always and in everything desire only his perfect pleasure, which ought to be yours. With a humble and patient love wait for his much desired return, and believe that this state is more profitable for you than you imagine. For it is by this means that the Beloved observes whether his Spouse is truly faithful or not.

But when the Spouse shows himself and actually becomes present to his bride, he fills its entire being, and makes it what he is. Without knowing how, it is suddenly so greatly dilated in the Beloved that it feels a wonderful simplicity and unity of spirit in its union with him. At such a time the soul should allow itself to be raised up and carried away without doing anything, except to follow the luminous and simple attraction of the Spouse who dwells within it.

The gibbet of love is experienced in two ways. In the *first*, after the soul has experienced the simple and moving attractions of the Divine Essence within it, it suddenly finds itself bound and hung up. After bestowing many caresses upon it, God is accustomed to test the work of his love by withdrawing the pleasure of his divine presence. The senses no longer enjoy his divine delights.

As a result the soul suffers painful agonies and even impatience, but with love. It's power to act seems to be suspended, and it is so profoundly absorbed that it finds it almost impossible to speak. Thus it is obliged to endure the great torments of love without remedy. For anything that it might do or others might do for it brings no consolation. Nor is it able even to desire consolation. The holiest and most exalted subjects bring no comfort.

Behold a soul in the throes of a grievous and painful death. Its own thoughts and those of others, no matter how elevated, are less than nothing compared to the supereminent Spirit whom it sees so ineffably. The soul is filled to overflowing with his infinite and loving immensity, and enjoys great lights and much love, but in a spirit of loving sorrow. In the deepest part of its being it is exceedingly joyful at seeing itself thus confined and attached to this gibbet of love, unable and unwilling to leave it.

The *second* way in which the soul finds itself suspended on the gibbet of love is far more painful than the first. Before this occurs the soul enjoys many luminous manifestations of the Divine Essence, and delightful and personal caresses. Love grows to such proportions that it gradually transforms the soul into the Divine Essence. The result is a profound union with the superessential Spirit which is above all being and non-being.

When the soul feels deprived of love and action, it soon falls into periods of sadness, anguish, sorrow and impatience. If it is not well instructed, it thinks that God no longer dwells in it and that it has lost the knowledge of him. When it least expects, it finds itself subject to great miseries, languors and deaths, and it feels that they are the just consequences of its loss of God and his divine caresses.

Nevertheless, when it sees that all means, both spiritual and temporal, fail it, it is willing to be forever afflicted and tormented on all sides, and even to be bound on this gibbet. What we have said here will serve as an infallible rule.

Every degree of love has its degree of infused illuminations, each one surpassing the other. If the soul perseveres in the practice of loving introversion, in time it will advance from the lowest to the highest and most eminent degree of love. But this practice demands an ardent and vigorous love, a love that is always at work, even amid suffering and death. It is a painful and yet an agreeable work of love. It has many stages and contrasting periods: periods of delight followed by privation, periods of sorrow and affliction, and periods of languor and grievous deaths. There are so many that it is impossible to describe them all. As the soul advances in these degrees of love, the periods of abandonment, privation and languor become more painful and seem to be almost intolerable. Perfect souls, when they see themselves deprived of the delights of luminous and radiant love, I mean God himself and his gifts, expire on crosses of grievous languors and endure agonizing sufferings more cruel than can be imagined.

There is an explanation for this. As the soul becomes filled with divine lights and delights, and thus gets to know the infinite love-ableness and excellence of God, its crosses accordingly become more grievous and painful when it is reduced to poverty and misery by the absence of its blessed Object. The least interval of disunion and sensible separation between these two subjects, so ravished with love for each other, is a cruel death to the soul. For now it lives and breathes only in the enjoyment of its Beloved.

Nevertheless, since it is wholly consumed and lost in love, and is now beyond all perception and enjoyment of its Well-Beloved, it willingly gives up this blessed delight in order to suffer and die on the gibbet of sensible separation for as long as he wishes. For the will of such a soul is so transformed into the will of God that we can no longer say there are two wills, but one, namely, the will of God alone. Thus it seeks only the divine will in its actions. And in periods of abandonment, poverty, agony and death it is always the will of God that it desires.

As for less perfect souls, their poverty, misery and languors correspond to the degree of infused and acquired love which they have attained, and the divine favors they have enjoyed. But the highest fidelity is required if they are to achieve the crown of all happiness. By this I mean the highest and the final degree of love, where the soul, by the continual practice of all we spoke of above, remains fixed and immoveable above itself and all things. Its own unity is transformed into him who draws and ravishes it to himself by the power of his alluring splendors, and by his infinite beauty, goodness and love.

(*Aspirations of a mystic soul*) O God of my heart, what are you doing? Are you thus forcing me gently, but freely, to love you? But how do you know whether I shall be happy in this? Ah! my Love, forgive me for what I am saying. See how these excesses deprive me of my judgment, and make me speak to your Majesty like a mad man? Oh, sweet, holy and loving compulsion! I feel myself so gently constrained that I resolve never to be separated from you even for a moment.

But you know, my Spouse, how creatures can stand in the way of our plans. Nevertheless, if you give them this power, it will not be for the purpose of harming me, but for my good, for my improvement. Only you my Beloved, can know how I desire to be alone with you, giving all for all.

Without you I have little interest in your gifts. As I belong completely to you, so do I want you to belong to me. My only wish is that you will possess me forever, that, in our simple love, we may become one and the same spirit.

Can there be anything more delightful to the lover than the constant sight and presence of his Well-Beloved, and only Love? This, O my One and All, is why your presence so transports me. It is a constant inspiration for love between us. What happiness for the spouse, to love and possess you thus! And you, how pleased you must be to enjoy your love without restraint. For the unique love of the Beloved constitutes the life and possessions of the lover. In the strength of their mutual love, the lover lives in tranquil and peaceful enjoyment of the Well-Beloved.

Henceforth, my Love, do not encumber me with your gifts, for I love you above every gift. Tell be, my Life, can we live apart from each other? No. You long for me with great love, and I too yearn for you with a most ardent love. But how shall we satisfy our yearning? Isn't it true, that the only thing you want me to do is to love? And whom do you want me to love, if not you? Oh, if only I were a seraph, so that I might the better correspond to your immense love!

Henceforth, whatever you do with me, or whatever you give me or take from me does not concern me, because I am in love with you. For me it is enough to be in love. I desire nothing more. And if I cannot always love you with the same fervor, your own love gives me assurance that I shall always desire you with the same hunger. Who will satisfy and nourish the beloved if not its Spouse? Moreover, I am confident that you will always be my food, and my hunger will be fully satisfied.

Ah Lord, do not be surprised if I say that I shall eat you. Is it not fitting that a spouse famished for love should feed on its Beloved? And you my Love, why do you consume me if you do not wish me to act in the same way toward you? Do you not know that it cannot be otherwise? Therefore, suffer what I have suffered, and am suffering according to the law of our mutual love. Is it not for this reason that you have fed me on ashes and reduced me to nothing without my being aware of it? If it is to devour and consume me that you have thus reduced me to nothing, then you should be quite content and that forever. What can be more just and fair? But why should a divine Being as excellent as you, act thus toward his creature, loving it in time and eternity, if not that each may enjoy the other in mutual love forever?

Let us leave the past and the present and look to the future. Where am I my Love? Where am I, if not in an age of misery and corruption? Still you have favored me, mortal and corruptible dust, with your love. So passionate a love have you bestowed on me that I cannot live for one moment without seeing you, speaking to you and feeling your presence. You are God, but a God of love who has smitten me with love for you. I am urged by such a gentle constraint that I am completely melted with joy and filled to satiety in you.

After this, how can I ever distrust you? If I did, I would be guilty of infidelity. And if I were to rely on myself, thinking that I could love you as I wished without your help, would not the angels and saints consider me mad? How could I even entertain such a thought, I who seek through love to consume flesh and blood in the fire of the greatest poverty of spirit, and in a constant and holy imitation of you?

You are within, my Love, and I too am there with you and will be there constantly. No, I will never look for you outside, for you are not there. Rather will I retire into the deepest center of my being, where I shall possess you in singular repose and delight. In this simple union, we shall take the greatest delight in each other. And I shall rejoice only in this that you are God. With this I am happy, completely satisfied that you are such, and that you will never be understood by any created being.

This intimate friendship of ours, my Love, urges me to love you alone forever. O God of my heart, since you are a God of love, I shall imitate you with an ardent, pure and naked love at all times: in suffering, in life and death. And if I should be so foolish as to withdraw from you in the most painful adversity, may I fail to sustain it. Indeed, that would be quite easy if you were to leave me alone and without you. But knowing by experience what you want me to be, I firmly believe that, when I am wholly plunged and lost in you, I shall be able to do all things in you. For you will comfort me in my most painful afflictions by a secret and divine support. Thus we shall live in each other constantly.

Ah! my Love, if it is such a blessed thing to feel you in the overflowing fullness of your love, for me it is an even more excellent thing to endure all things, even to die in you and for you. I call you to witness, my Beloved, whether the present life is sweet for me. Without you I would by necessity be constantly filled with sorrow and regret.

O my Lord, what a sad thing it is to see myself subject to such a cruel and troublesome enemy as my body. It not only hinders the full satisfaction of my famished desire, but also drags me down to the earth and to corruption, so much so, that it often makes me succumb to the cruelty of its demands under pretext of a just and reasonable necessity. And what is worse, I am never done with it. Why is it so, my Love? And why do you not allow me to afflict it by waging war upon it?

Ah! my Lord, I know why you do not permit it. The principal reason is that the conflict I am enduring through my body and my feeble resistance to it, in spite of my best effort, is a subject for constant renunciation. One thing I know to be very true, namely, that it is far more noble to imitate you and constantly follow you in spirit than to be lost in you without such imitation. But a soul that is passionately in love with you as I am, possesses all things, does all things and endures all things. It dies constantly because of its love for you.

For this reason you fill all my faculties with your Being and your love. I see you and possess you more delightfully than I can possibly describe, or even dare to say. Since my complete transfusion into you, you alone know how intimate are our communings and our actions, and how they express the most profound love, consolation and joy of our mutual union. Ah! my Love, you know it only too well, for it is you who do this according to your pleasure. But if it were to last for any length of time, I would die on the instant. So then, I would die of love. What is it to die of love in you who are love? Ah! Beloved, it would be a death that is all too delightful and happy! Such is not your wish, nor mine, for I desire to be conformed to you.

Tell me, my Life, why have you given me your Word, if not to let me know that I must not aspire to such a delightful death? Therefore, it is enough for me to die of a love that finds its consummation in the two of us. For this reason I want to follow your Incarnate Word through all the desert paths which he traversed with such great love throughout his life up to his death.

O Lord, my God, you who made everything for me, and made me for you, I wish to love you infinitely. But without you and without your grace I cannot love you. Then too, in order to destroy my vices and imperfections and to clothe myself with your Spirit, I have an infinite need of your grace. I need it also in order to give you pleasure by the constant practice of humility and all the other virtues.

Therefore, when some humiliation presents itself, I will receive it, not as coming from creatures, but as a very special gift from your generous and fatherly hand. I will only look upon creatures as the ministers and instruments you have selected from all eternity to exercise me in hatred of myself through every kind of mortification. And the one purpose of it all is that you may rule happily and gloriously in me forever, that you may rejoice in all my thoughts, works and omissions.

With the help of your grace, O my God, I will never deliberately become upset when I fail to keep my good resolutions, even though I fail frequently. Left to myself, I cannot do otherwise than fall, and without you I would not know how to rise up again. As much as I distrust myself, so much do I trust in you, my Savior.

My God and my All, I know that you are infinitely more aware of me than I am of myself. But as for me, unless I love you with all my strength, I shall not be sufficiently conscious of you, that is, for your glory and my own good. Considering my weakness and nothingness, I tremble when I think how formidable a task it is for me. Still, since it is a question of your interests and not mine, I have nothing to fear. What reason have I for distrusting you from whom I have received so many favors?

Therefore, when I sensibly enjoy your love and your presence, I shall speak to you constantly out of the abundance of my heart. And when I am in aridity and no longer enjoy these favors, I shall never turn to anyone else but to you. Nor shall I give way to anxiety or useless examinations. But I will speak to you as much as I am able. If I cannot even speak to you, then I shall suffer you and patiently sustain you as long as you wish. This way of acting will open my mind and heart so as to dilate me in the abundance of your divine Spirit. All that I see and understand I shall adapt to this simple action in order to avoid being sterile. In you I shall occupy myself with the truths and affectionate incentives that your Majesty will always furnish in abundance.

I will especially open my heart fully and lovingly to your bitter Passion, transforming it as much as possible into very affectionate and loving conversations. Not only shall I exercise myself in love, but I shall also practice all the virtues, for they are, as it were, the body, while love is the soul of the perfect life. When it is acquired by the practice of all the virtues, love becomes very exalted and perfect, and enables the soul to live in you most happily.

I desire only you, my divine Love, only you. When I am sick, you will be my health. When I am weak, you will be my strength. When my soul or even my body is in darkness, (*remember, he was blind*) you will be my light. When I am hungry, you will be my fullness. When I am cold, you will be my warmth, or better, my burning and consuming fire. All that I need, I shall possess most abundantly in your actual presence. This I shall enjoy through frequent and humble occupation with you.

Most of all I love to be occupied with you alone, rather than with your divine works. All these I accept on faith, but leave them as they are in order to be with you alone.

Ah! my Love, isn't it true that all is love, like an effect springing from its cause? The earth and all the universe is love. All is full of love. And in all places you are constantly performing works of love. How admirable are the most lofty thoughts and intelligences of love, your angels! How exalted and ardent are your Seraphim! And men of love, how passionately in love are they with Divine Love!

O Spouse of souls, why have you made us capable of love? Why have you filled us with love? Was it not that we might be wounded in every part of our being by the most keen darts of your love? Indeed, you delight in discharging them by the thousands against us, so that we shall inevitably be wounded by them and love you madly with a simple and unique love. O Love, you flood all who are within you, and yet not everyone is inundated or lost in your torrents. But he is engulfed in you who is disposed for it and wants it. As for me, I am submerged and wholly lost in you, not to die, but to live solely in you and by you. For you are the life of my life, a divinely vivifying life. You are the love that engulfs and consumes, the love that produces love, impassioning the lover to love you with your own love.

O my Love, I wish that I may never again give in to sin, passion, evil actions or inclinations. And never consent to voluntary dissimilarities with you, or with what you are, be it ever so little.

Why was I created, my Beloved, if not to love you above your gifts, and to become love through love? O Love, I desire you and you alone, not your gifts.

What you are, that I too wish to be through love, namely, sovereignly and infinitely in love with you, who love yourself divinely, perfectly and infinitely. Your love and joy are equal to what you are, equal to your exceedingly infinite and divine Nature, which thus enjoys perpetual happiness. It penetrates and anticipates all that you are, all that you know and desire without limit. It is beyond the comprehension of the most exalted intelligence of men and angels, and of all possible creatures.

O love, love, true love, eternal love, infinite love! You are all powerful, able to do not only great things, but even to change love through love, so that thereafter, the soul becomes ardently impassioned with love in love itself, namely, in you.

Alas! My Life and my Love, what pleasure and happiness can I ever have except in seeing, knowing and loving you, and in being supremely in love with you. If only men knew and felt this truth! How quickly and easily would they leave themselves in order to know and love you alone for all eternity.

But, my eternal and infinite Spouse, you have some very select spouses, chosen with a very special and particular love. It is my great happiness to belong to you as one of this number. Why have I been chosen, my Love, if not to become love? Yes, to destroy my self-love, in order to live in you. Thus, through you, for you and in you, I am to become love.

Then too, why have you hidden yourself in me in your incarnate Majesty, and again in another manner within my soul? Did you not know that I would be so wounded by such love that I would have to spend the rest of my poor life in a painful languor without any relief or consolation?

Ah! How miserable and unhappy is my lot, since my exile from you is so cruelly prolonged! Who will deliver me quickly from this mortal body, and put an end to my languors by granting me the eternal possession of you, my infinite love?

No, no, my Life, in this matter I see neither past nor future. For now I have become you. I have become enamored of love through love. All is lost in you, in a state of loving and being loved.

Of what importance is it to know what I am and who I am? Or to know what may happen to me, as long as I become love through loving? How happy is the spouse who has attained this by its fidelity! For now it will never be separated from its love. Tell me, my Life, why have you espoused me, if not for this purpose? How many are the favors you have bestowed upon me for this reason! Shall I not use them all to be your loyal and faithful spouse?

O Angels, you now enjoy my Love in the fullness of his glory. He overwhelms you with love, joy and happiness. While you are consumed with joy in him, I must continue in this sad and painful life, fighting against a host of enemies in order to possess my Love in love.

O my Beloved, will you leave me here much longer to languish

with love? Why do you not redouble the infusion of your love
so that I, your most unworthy spouse, may be destroyed and changed
into you. Why don't you dilate my heart so that it may have an
infinite desire for you and thus contain you? Now, what am I
saying? Have I not this capacity? Who will deny it when he sees
me so reduced and consumed by my desire for love? No, no, my
Love, I have this capacity because you are my Spouse, my Love
and my All.

Is it not your wish, O my Beloved, to transform your spouse
into love itself? Since I belong to you and my whole being is a
wound of love, I shall never live without you or outside of you.
Pardon me my love. I wish to say that I shall never voluntarily
live in my own love (*self-love*), without your love or outside of
your love. Nor shall I ever cease to love you actively more and
more until I finally die of love.

Ah! How little are you known, how little desired, how little
appreciated, savored and loved! Forgive me. I am foolish and,
in the excess of my love, I do not know what I am saying. I should
say, how you are known, desired, faithfully loved and happily
possessed! No, I do not seek you just for myself. In the midst
of your gifts I wish to possess only you without your gifts, and
for yourself.

(*Transforming union*)   In this state these two spirits (viz. *God and
the mystic soul*) engage in a combat of love in which there is an
exchange of loving glances, and a glitter of incomparable light,
all done for their own mutual pleasure and happiness. Neither of
these loving spirits wants to give up in this struggle of mutual,
loving embraces, until the weakest of the two finally considers
himself vanquished, and sees himself fall irrevocably into the infinite
immensity of his eternal Object. There, seeing himself surrounded
on all sides by his Beloved and by his divine attributes, he plunges
into him, and is lost and dilated in him with a joy and happiness
that exceed all human understanding.

Here, the union of these two lovers becomes one and unique,
and is above perfect union. The two spirits dissolve into one spirit.
As I have said, this union is above the common and ordinary union.

The latter is achieved by a love that is indeed lively, effective and ardent, but it is active only in the ordinary manner. However, the soul that has arrived at sovereign perfection by a simple and active fidelity, tastes the profound simplicity of God by experience. It sees that their common enjoyment is the Paradise of God in the soul.

My Beloved, I have not told you how I intend to revenge myself upon you for the sweet and loving warfare that you constantly wage upon me. If you rejoice in the acts of profound love with which you constantly favor me, then I too will constantly come to you in the strength of my love. Thus there will be a mutual and frequent encounter of spirit with spirit, until one of us is vanquished. But what am I saying? Pardon me this excess, my Love. I mean, until I, in love and strength, have succumbed to your infinite strength and love. Thus, completely conquered, I shall thereafter let myself be entirely inspired and possessed by you without any possible resistance.

1. Cf. glossary.

CHAPTER V

UNION OF THE INTERIOR LIFE WITH THE ACTIVE LIFE[1]

How to perform external work

If we are not busy in active work, we should give our time to recollection and occupation with God. When we are called by obedience to assist our neighbor, we must perform our task in keeping with all the demands of this virtue. To do it well and to converse with spiritual profit, we must preserve our religious bearing and not adopt a worldly manner. We should be serious and dignified in our manner and conversation; prudent, calm and understanding, always leaving others free to speak, providing they do so seriously and becomingly. If their conversation is scandalous and they are persons of rank, we should discreetly draw them away from such talk and introduce a more serious topic. If they persist in this vein despite prudent efforts on our part, we should gently reprove them if we think it will do any good; if not, we should show a pained expression, thus indicating our displeasure. However, let us use every means possible to engage them in some serious conversation.

Strange, how many worldly persons, even those of high station, are not afraid to shock us. They have no respect for our state. However, this evil is often due to the fact that we are not sufficiently serious in our speech and our actions, and are too willing to listen to good and evil alike. Thus their evil tongues empty the scum of their hearts into our own. And God grant that we may not be influenced by it through a false, sensual freedom, to take pleasure in remembering it and relating it to others. What a disgrace it would be to use this filth in order to keep up our conversation, or to find religious so reckless in their speech and gestures that the worldly-minded would look upon them as good clowns. They might even be deeply disedified by them. This is said merely in passing so that we may avoid these snares of the world like death itself. They are detested even by serious-minded lay people.

Good religious carefully avoid this evil. Deep in their hearts they carry the thought and image of our Savior, and often fly to him by means of a loving inclination. There, in his divinity, they are detained, by a simple and naked contemplation of his essence, his infinite perfections and the mysteries of our faith. And when they perform external works, they do so without leaving him, for they look very attentively at his Humanity and are accompanied by his holy Presence. Consequently, when they are among men, and even among sinners, they always speak with wisdom Thus they imitate our Lord Who also performed external works when necessity or his own infinite love demanded it.

But since we are infinitely removed from his perfection, we should always have a certain fear for what is external, because, only with great difficulty can our powers be occupied with God and external things at the same time. Hence, we must frequently recollect our hearts in God and not burden ourselves unduly with external things. If we do this, we shall be detached and thus will perform our external actions as if we were not actually performing them. With our senses thus dead to their purely animal function, our soul will be more vigorous and consequently far removed from these things. But if we have not yet attained such perfection, we can at least make use of a spiritual practice that will protect us from evil images and impressions.

In some religious communities[2] the superior, using flimsy reasons and pretexts, may be excessively inclined to send his religious out into active work. But the true spirit of Carmel is as much opposed to this as fire is to water, and day to night. Let him who wishes, hear and understand. This is a trap.

"God," says St. Gregory, "prevents his children from loving external works too much. He acts like the father of a family who trains his servants to do the work from which he exempts his children. His Majesty tests his children by means of crosses and spiritual tribulations, while the servants are heavily weighed down to the earth." (cf. St. Gregory, 25, *Moralia*) O God! What are we to think and say of this? O Superiors, look into your consciences and see if you are imitating God in this matter. Seek the greatest good for your children. Frequently give them the spiritual food they need for their weakness, either yourselves or at least through someone chosen by you. And do it wisely so that you may not have to render an account to God for your cowardice and negligence. Help each one according to his need. For even if you act with the greatest circumspection in this matter, you will scarcely be doing your duty. Remember, the life of man is short. God alone and his truth endure eternally.

As for religious, they should have no inordinate fear of external works. But superiors should be careful not to overburden them or draw them into such activity without good reason. However, if the religious doesn't want to undertake such activity at all, he must be forced to do so. He must be compelled to perform such work within the monastery, until he has learned to find God equally everywhere. Still, if a particular religious has no aptitude for external things, he should be left in solitude, and only be drawn outside as little as possible. This is to be applied not only to the most spiritual, but also to beginners, because solitude is our aim, and it leads directly to our final end.

As for those who are neither suited for solitude nor for the contemplative life, superiors should employ them in external assignments. Since perfect solitaries will always be very few in number, they should carefully avoid overloading them with external activities which are opposed to what is of real, lasting benefit as well as to the best part of our spirit. This is a mistake which I have deplored elsewhere. Certainly it will be a great misfortune when superiors no longer make any distinction between those who are born for external things and those who are not. When there seems to be no remedy for this evil, see to it, O religious souls, that you carry your solitude everywhere with you by means of a constant and active fidelity. By so doing, you will experience great things, for you will become aware of God's frequent entries into you, and of yourself into God.

There are four things you should carefully practice in external works. *First,* whether they are works of pure obedience or of your own choice, you should perform them promptly and quickly, in order to preserve the simple unity of your spirit. Your soul will know this by experience when, through practice and fidelity, it has acquired a simple intention and is able to give constant attention to its divine Object. The *second* rule is that you should never consider any misfortune or accident as coming from creatures, but rather from the most pure and generous hand of God. This attitude will have great influence in keeping you patient and tranquil at all times, and in all difficulties. Thus you will always preserve union with God. The *third* rule is that you should see all things in their true light and essence, and not as they appear to be. In this way you will never be troubled. The *fourth* rule is that you should carefully avoid burdening yourself with an unnecessary solicitude for the affairs of others which do not concern you. Even in cases which concern you by reason of your office, you must conduct yourself prudently and preserve peace of soul. As much as possible, never allow yourself to become disturbed over them.

When you have some external work to do, carefully avoid becoming attached to it. Let your heart be involved only to the extent that is necessary to perform it well. You must perform such work with a reasonable fear of becoming too attached to it and of being entangled by it after it is completed. Do not look for things to do, unless they are duties of your state.

Always be even tempered and joyful, and complete master of yourself. Carefully watch your thoughts and actions, and, as much as possible, avoid giving in to any interior or exterior disorder arising from some sudden, slight disturbance or indiscretion. Moreover, know what you are doing and why you do it. By this means the interior and exterior man will become an excellent temple of the living God, full of spiritual treasures. And it will always appear as such to the great edification both of yourself as well as of those with whom you are conversing.

We must not be content just to live a good moral life. We must live a holy life in this place of exile, uniting ourselves lovingly to God as often as possible, even amid the greatest distractions. We must believe, as an article of faith, that nothing is more essential and important than that. While it is true that obedience is of more value than sacrifice, still when we undertake external works through obedience we should do so without deserting our interior. We should preserve a simple intention and attention. These keep us to a certain extent suspended in and attached to God, our final Object, by means of a simple desire. Thus we are able to remain united to him quite simply and nakedly during our occupations. For this reason we should carefully avoid fulfilling acts of obedience merely out of natural pleasure and eagerness under pretext of obeying promptly and easily. It is never necessary to perform external actions with such eagerness and desire that we are completely drawn out of ourselves.

It is quite sufficient if we perform external tasks with only the attention they need to be done well. And when we see that our whole interior has been scattered abroad, it is a sign that we have no interior spirit, and no acquired virtue, that we are living only in nature and in the senses. Although we perform holy tasks, we do so only on a natural, sensible and external plane. If we constantly thought of God in a loving manner, and kept this as our principal aim and deepest desire, we would at the same time be able to keep an eye on ourselves. We would admire the beauty and excellence of the spirit of our Order, a spirit which ought to animate the whole body of the Order, and the smallest things done within it. Seeing it, we would want to acquire it, and preserve it in all the glory of its perfection, completely surrendered to God for his greatest glory.

If we live thus in truth and reality, and not just in appearance, we will taste the delights of such a life. Moreover, we will realize how important it is to leave God for God's sake, that is, to leave him in the things that concern us and our own satisfaction in order to follow him in and for himself. Here we will also see how acts of complete, perfect and constant self-abandonment are infinitely more exalted and perfect than acts which we ourselves have planned. These latter are a source of self-satisfaction, to which we are often subtly attached without even knowing it. Moreover, the shortest path that we can take is the interior path. Our spirit should never relax in the smallest degree in its exercise of love. This activity, however, should be above the senses. By this means the soul often plunges itself deeply into God, its Object and repose. In this it is like the fish that plunges into the water where it seeks its own element, its center and repose.

God expects us to leave ourselves and, in obedience to the superior, to undertake external works according to our state and condition. If the circumstances require manual work, it should be done holily as something ordered by God. While we apply our body to the task, our mind should rest sweetly in the loving bosom of God. Now we must carefully avoid working with too much eagerness. This will not happen, if the soul is already quite recollected and lost in God. Then the lower man is subject to the spirit, and therefore, all the actions of the senses belong to the spirit. This state is so simple and one that has the power to enrapture the soul from within. Thus it no longer feels any opposition between one or the other of these parts (i.e., *the senses and the spirit*).

Guard against becoming attached to what you see and hear, so that you may preserve freedom of heart and detachment from forms and images. Failure here would be a great weakness and spiritual defect, especially if you go looking for such things. But if, perchance, you find yourself engaged in them by obedience, leave them on the outside as something unworthy of you, which you abhor like death itself. Nevertheless, you must leave God for God's sake, and you will lose nothing by it, because your soul can be so recollected in him that all these things, while impressing the senses, in no way enter the soul itself. Hence, with very little mental effort, you can refuse entrance to them and yet, while such a task lasts, you can remain as attentive to God within, as if nothing happened. True, this supposes that the soul has already practiced this exercise for a long time. Attachment to forms and images is the greatest difficulty encountered by beginners. It is there that they go to ruin because of their immoderation.

When you have something very important to do, do not hesitate to use all your industry in order to do it well. But it will be wise to spend some time studying the ways to do it. After that leave the care of it to God without giving it any further thought. If you are simultaneously busy with a number of important tasks (*he is speaking to the Bishop of Dol*) study the way to perform each of them in particular. Do not consider them all at one time, inasmuch as this would be confusing, and would overburden you with an infinite number of distractions. Having done this, leave the matter to God who will bring all to a successful conclusion, to his own greater good and glory.

Since the vicissitudes of human affairs often oblige us to undertake external work, he who is deeply recollected is consequently often obliged to leave his repose and sweetness. But he never leaves in such a way that he loses it, for the liberty of mind and heart which he enjoys, enables him to re-enter there frequently. As a result such a person works only with his body, and is not attached to his occupation. Nor is he ever distracted in the enjoyment of his paradise, unless it be for a very brief interval. Here we also wish to include souls who are most perfect in the practice of contemplative love. Such souls must not be assigned to external things, except it be according to the rules we have given elsewhere.

(*For advanced souls*) We should apply our mind and attention to the performance of external things as much as is necessary to do them well, without worrying about being distracted. Otherwise, we should only be concerned about the desires of our Spouse, which ought to be our own, seeking to unite our will completely to his. Thus we shall dwell in intimate union with him, immoveable and well-ordered, prepared to act, suffer and die in God-likeness.

From this we can see quite clearly how disloyal it is to relax our attention ever so little, and to diminish our activity toward God, when we are recollected. But when we are very busy externally, in order to withdraw within ourselves, we should use simple glances and acts which, by their power, draw all the faculties of the soul to their beloved Object. There you have the means of performing activity holily, both interiorly and exteriorly.

In order to preserve the happiness of God's favor and a simple adherence to him, interior souls maintain a continual occupation with his divine Majesty. All external tasks of obligation are done promptly and diligently. When they are done quickly it may be taken as a sure sign of an interior soul. Here I am only speaking of such souls and not of those who live entirely in the senses and without devotion. Now the reason why interior souls do not seek external activity and perform it quickly when they undertake it is because their love is in the deepest part of their being, and because they fear being influenced by the images and thoughts of what is done or said in long-winded conversations. This would divide the spirit and deflect it from the simple and interior unity, in which it enjoys a singular peace and repose that are above the thoughts and images of creatures.

(*To act in God and to act for God are two different things*) Let your activity be gentle, moderate and controlled, not affected, but always modest and performed in the sight of God who sees you. Do not set your heart on what you do with your hands and your body, but have a reasonable interest in it and your bodily labor will suffice. If you follow these recommendations you will not be influenced by external images.

On this matter, my Beloved, I hold that it is far more exalted and profitable to act in you, than to act for you. In the first instance, the intention is simple. Here the soul does not look so much at the works it performs, as it looks at you in whom it performs them. On the other hand, a soul concerned with a right and pure intention pays more attention to its works in order to perform them faithfully and well, than to you for whom it undertakes them. Hence, these works become obstacles between you and the human heart. But works that are done in you are free of these impediments inasmuch as the soul in this state (already quite advanced, and beyond the senses) is able to penetrate right to God in all its works without being hindered by forms and images. Such acts, O my Love, are done quickly, simply and exceptionally well, and with great wisdom and unction. This is possible because the simple eye of the understanding is now able to contemplate you with great purity and simplicity. Thus, in a moment, the soul is able to anticipate and penetrate the whole exterior of what is presented to it. The other intention which is not yet simple, but only pure and sincere, is greatly influenced by forms and images. These affect the heart, and fill it with a great many reflections, divisions, fears, and sudden surprises. And although this condition exists in varying degrees, some effects of it will always remain in the soul as long as it does not advance beyond the first kind of intention.

(*Conversation*) When we lose the remembrance of God which flows from the simple and joyful inclination of the spirit into the senses, do we also lose that very simple and fixed glance by which we are cast into God? My answer is that we can disturb the interior senses so much and for such a long time when we are speaking of matters that are rather indifferent or even very good and holy that we may lose the remembrance of God entirely. And during that time we may be lost only in the senses. Thus, it is quite likely that we may not only fall into imperfection, but even into sin. But when the soul is in no way attached to such things, it not only does not lose its view and remembrance of God, but it is even more profoundly enraptured and transformed in its super-essential unity.

   Those who feel the need to be constantly talking are very much deceived. For, in the course of their conversation, they find themselves under such compulsion that they have hardly anything to contribute to it. Little by little they lose the presence of God. Under thinly disguised pretexts they throw themselves into all kinds of affairs. And after having spent the day in such activities, they find themselves as devoid of God's presence as the unfortunate worldlings. All this is due to the fact that they have allowed themselves to be allured by the sweetness and delight of their natural spirit, thinking they would be able to recollect themselves whenever they wished. But they find the contrary to be the case, for they see themselves hindered and caught in the snares of their own nature.

   Note and practice with great prudence the saying of the Wise Man, that we should answer the foolish person according to his foolishness. Such a line of conduct is part of perfect prudence and the religious who is interiorly recollected with God will infallibly follow it. For God will not allow him to be wanting either in experience or in practice amid these dangerous snares. He will always avoid them with tranquility and freedom of spirit.

Good religious are not deceived by the pretty and honeyed words of the worldly. From the very beginning they maintain great recollection, and therefore, these flatteries have no influence on them. Within they are firmly established in God and thus can act with prudence during their conversation without any great harm to their perfection.

It is difficult for simple souls to converse well with seculars, because they must be drawn out of themselves and away from their simple and unique repose. Then they are obliged to accommodate themselves to the low level of those with whom they associate and to their conversations which are carried on with much difficulty and disquiet. Simple souls, since they enjoy a simple light and a unique simplicity, experience great difficulty and uneasiness in thus accommodating themselves to these minds which are crowded with thoughts and images. On these subjects they are without forms (or, *ideas*). All such souls, who are new at conversation with seculars, experience this difficulty. The only rule we can give is, if it is not necessary, they should quite simply avoid using their reason to investigate such subjects of conversation.

Saving better advice, we should not mortify or try anyone, no matter how lowly he may be, unless we have the authority. For we ought to be withdrawn from all that we can see and hear. Nevertheless, we are not forbidden to speak of holy things and to exhort our neighbor to piety and to his duty, according to occasions.

In private conversation with religious of our own Order we should accommodate ourselves to their ways for the moment, so that we may be able to console and edify them. Then, too, we should not be too serious or reserved, otherwise we may be burdensome and annoying to them. However, we should not follow this procedure with other religious, especially if they are quite ordinary. With them we should be as serious and as modest as if we were alone with God. For their edification and liberty we should let them do and say what they like and at the same time keep a serene and smiling countenance of approval. From time to time we should make an opportune reply to the subject they are discussing. But if they are too set on talking for their own pleasure, after some time, we should politely take leave of them, giving as our excuse the fact that we have something to do at that moment, which is by no means a lie.

When we are in the company of those who are higher in rank than we are, we should let them choose the subjects of conversation. For our part we should be content to raise objections and give replies with skill and prudence, but should never contradict them. Such people will brook no opposition or contradiction. It is very important for us to know how to conceal our feelings at such a time, even though the things discussed are obviously unpleasant.

(*Studies*)   As for the sciences, it is very difficult to devote oneself to them without prejudice to divine wisdom, because there is great opposition between the one and the other. In itself divine wisdom is simple and single and confers the same qualities on the soul that possesses it. Through it the powers of the soul are reformed and easily disposed for complete union with God. The sciences on the other hand introduce multiplicity into the soul and make its approach to God very difficult.

Therefore to preserve this wisdom during studies, the soul must cultivate an intimate desire always to adhere to God by a simple, joyful inclination, and to the knowledge and certainty that God exists. At the same time, it should exercise self-control, and often unite its whole being to this God of the sciences and of the virtues. This does not mean that, during actual study, the soul should always feel God flowing into its faculties, filling and drawing them to himself. It is sufficient if it performs this action without complete gratification and natural satisfaction, and without making an end of it. On the other hand, it does not mean that the sciences should in no way touch or delight the soul, for there ought to be a moderate delight in them, somewhat like the delight of well-born and spiritual persons when eating and drinking. They perform this action out of necessity and for their well-being rather than for sensual pleasure.

In this as in everything else the soul must obey above all out of love for God. It should carefully guard against performing this or any other work away from God's presence, no matter how laborious it may be. Let it perform all tasks in the same way that it performs simple exercises of love which are interior, tasteful and simple. For the soul that is touched by an ardent love for God there is no distinction between outside and inside. And although it may feel itself greatly multiplied and distracted by external occupations in spite of itself, still it must endure this painful battle, and sacrifice itself by means of short aspirations. These should be launched toward God with all its heart, at least for the space of an *Ave Maria*.

(*Advice to advanced souls on external work*) Very few undertake active work with the right spirit, because they are afraid to lose their delightful repose. Such an attitude shows blindness and ignorance, because action infallibly perfects and deepens the soul's contemplation and enjoyment of its divine Object, providing it exercises a complete interior and exterior custody over itself. Moreover, by abandoning itself always and in everything the soul achieves a simple repose in God which is proof against all opposition from the senses.

Besides, such conflicts between the spirit and the senses plunge the soul deep into God, although it actually thinks these abandonments and wars withdraw it from him. In truth, they are the reason for it being all the more profoundly absorbed and transformed into him. For God, being what he is, is infinitely distant from our feelings. Consequently, the feelings of delight that we experience concerning him withdraw us from him. And the more we think we are in God and please him by such feelings, the more we are in ourselves. On the other hand, although it may be imperceptible to us and contrary to our senses, our acts of abandonment to God plunge us very deeply into him.

Meanwhile, let us remain tranquil, simple and vigilant, keeping our eye constantly fixed on our divine Object. And let us not give up transitory things at the wrong time. They will not have a bad effect on us if we are indeed spiritually dead. Such we must be in order to live in perpetual contemplation of God above the senses and the understanding, and beyond admiration. Through the exercise of a moderate, mental control, let us strive to become so simple and tranquil within that, as far as we are able, we do not allow our thoughts to stray or our spirit to be divided ever so little by the images of the imagination.

When we become aware of such wanderings and divisions of spirit, we must check them without using formal acts. Instead we should exercise interior restraint by means of a very simple inclination and desire. For if some passion should be inordinately aroused or a temptation becomes quite strong within us, it is for God to dispel it when it shall please him, and not us, since it is he who now lives in us and not we ourselves. And it will not be wrong to say that it is God who endures it in our created being. Therefore, it is for him to do with it what he pleases, without our being otherwise disturbed over it. (Note: *He is speaking here of mystic souls who are truly dead to self, and enjoy a very close union with God.*)

(*How to regain a recollected spirit when disturbed and distracted.*) When you have performed some action that disturbs your senses for a long time, after it is completed, carefully avoid speaking to anyone immediately under any pretext whatever. Wait until the disturbing influence has passed and you have recovered that intimate awareness of God in your spirit, and the simple light of enlightened reason. Then, when your mind and senses have attained a certain degree of tranquility, you will once more be able to take up your work without fear of danger.

(*Those who are too active and opposed to the interior life*) Such persons are content to roam about in external things. Since they live only on the outside, it is there that they put all their perfection. Hence, they are continually occupied in active works, full of formalities and ceremonies, even busy about things of no importance. So great is their esteem for such a life that they despise those who are not active like themselves. But in reality under the appearance of goodness, they are running away from interior recollection at a gallop. To live thus opposed to the interior life is to lock the door to the spiritual life. As long as they glory in external things, they will continue to ignore this life. And the more they increase these useless formalities in order to acquire or to avoid something, the more impossible it becomes to know themselves spiritually, in naked and luminous simplicity, and in perfect detachment and recollection.

Finally, those who live in external things seek themselves in all that they do. All their activities are the product of an imagination conformed to their many appetites. They are continually lost in pleasant dreams over their plans and their works. As for their desires, they strive with might and main to satisfy them, no matter what the cost, even at the expense of others. Such then are the labors of those who are carried away and ruled by pride and self-love. From it come all sin and corruption, both of soul and body. And if the actions of the best of them do not go that far, which is rather doubtful, we can at least say that their work is only dross and a loss of time.

Ordinarily we must not force religious to do what is contrary to their ability, as long as they exercise it usefully for the common good and for their neighbor. But such a talent must not be merely imaginary, for then they would be doing their own will in all things rather than God's will. In that case their whole life would be nothing else than a constant expression of self-seeking, a life in which they deny nothing to their senses and their desires. Thus, where religious of former centuries were eager to submit to their superiors, these religious are just as eager to free themselves from their obedience and their direction. Their life is more characteristic of wayward souls, rather than of souls who want to die to self. Being quite full of themselves, they do only what seems good to them, without remorse of conscience and in spite of their knowledge and learning.

Actually some of them seem to be obsessed with the desire for knowledge. But this only leads to their confusion. For, while they should perform their task of instructing and assisting their neighbor, it is always accessory to their religious profession. He who is in his center is in repose, and he who is not there has no repose. So the repose of a religious ought to be found within and not outside. But the religious under discussion have hardly any experience or appreciation of this, even though they spend some time in meditation. Actually they spend as little time as possible in it,

and yet think they have sufficiently satisfied their obligation. The
rest of the time is wasted in a feverish desire to be out in external
affairs. The regular life and their own spiritual good are no concern
of theirs. But since they have neither heart nor desire to strive
for that good, how can they acquire it?

(*He is speaking of religious who are very worldly. They go everywhere without necessity and become involved in many unnecessary
activities.*) All we can do in such a case is to deplore it and to
give those motivated by the best intentions the advice of a holy
Father, "Work, seclusion and voluntary poverty are the marks of
good religious. This is what brings honor and glory to monasteries."
When necessity obliges us to converse with others, let us remember
these words of Hugh of St. Victor, "When you are constrained by
necessity to go outside the monastery, let the manliness of your
habit, the simplicity of your countenance, the innocence of your
life and the holiness of your conversation be a devout instruction
to others." This is the way we must edify our neighbor. Man is a
plant that is turned upside down and must bear fruit quite differently from insensible plants. First of all, he should bear abundant
fruit for himself, then he will bear sufficient fruit for others. But
the religious of whom I am speaking here do just the contrary.
They act like the other fruit-bearing plants of nature which bring
no good to themselves by their fruits, but only to others. Hence,
it is a great pity that those who ought to be trees of life for themselves, especially in the religious state, in their own case often
bear fruits of death, even as they strive to benefit others.

    What shall we do then? Shall we go to the other extreme? No.
But I venture to say that, unless we prudently approach extremes
to some extent, we shall never find the golden mean wherein true
virtue and real goodness dwell. But fear of going to this kind of
excess is not what holds these religious back. What deters them
is that they do not want perfection when it is bought at such a
high price. But if the first religious had not had such a desire,
the Church would not have such a great number of saints today
in all the religious orders. Their perfect lives are set before us as
so many mirrors, so that we might imitate them according to our

ability. Is it not a pity to see religious who, because they have no love for recollection, yield to idleness when they are not occupied in study or some external work? For them recollection is a waste of time. How can we expect to find virtuous persons among them, since their desire is so contrary to the source of all virtue, namely, recollection and prayer.

If this were the only evil that existed in the monasteries of such religious it would be bad enough. For he who has no love for interior solitude is necessarily the plaything and the target of all his evil desires. And when he gives in to them, he commits as much evil as he is capable of. Such religious are weak bodies in the cloister, while their souls roam over land and sea. Not knowing themselves, they become slaves to a multitude of unknown evils. They devote themselves to building programs and similar projects. To them we might apply these words of a holy Father, "The monks build monasteries for themselves in order to keep the external man under custody, but would to God that they built them in order to keep the interior man under regular discipline." Thus does he deplore the state of certain religious of his time, foreseeing that they might become even more imperfect in the future.

Now I do not mean that we should create a religious order whose members, without exception, must be animated by the purest interior spirit. But I say that they should at least be inspired by a spirit of moral integrity and virtue, while a certain number of them will be, more or less, inspired by divine wisdom. Thus everything would go far better than it does. Regularity would be wonderfully restored. The order would be indefatigable in its works and its struggles, and each member would feel the weight of his burden less.

He who is not spiritual and does not have virtuous habits that are perfectly acquired by the practice of their acts, is a religious only in name. Such a religious is naked and stripped of the weapons he needs to carry on a constant warfare against himself. For he cannot acquire the habits of the new man according to justice, virtue and holiness, except by destroying his old habits. Thus, to some extent at least, he is disposed for complete reform. Hence, we must use force and violence, and delight in laboring and suffering for the pure glory of God. If we act thus with unfailing perseverance, we shall finally acquire the virtues as habits withot thinking of it.

Religious place themselves in great spiritual danger when they prefer what is accidental to what is essential in the spirit of their Order. Every evil arises from gadding about under pretext of assisting one's neighbor. Alas! What a shame to ignore the real good and want to save the whole world at the cost of one's salvation. All enter religious life to save themselves, but soon the longing to achieve eminence in the sciences takes hold of them. They want, so they say, to procure the salvation of their neighbor. But they do so by neglecting their own. One day they will see what little good will come to them for having used the gifts of God only to satisfy their desires under the pretext of charity. What actually is left them of the spirit of their first founders and patriarchs? Indeed, although they may be their children, they possess no vestige of their spirit, because that which is accidental has taken it away from them. They reach such a point that they cannot even endure the renewal of this spirit in their brothers, although God does not fail to preserve it in some of them. But the others are so opposed to it that these good souls are obliged to remain hidden. They seem to live like the others in order to have peace. But secretly they remain faithful in the Spirit of God.

Of what use is it to have a set of excellent rules, when religious despise what they enjoin, namely, the love of solitude, continual occupation with God, meditation on his divine Law and a pure and clean heart. But this is what they most abhor. And yet they boast of the excellence of their Order without wishing to observe the rules which their Fathers left them. In this they are like the ordinary person, who, while loving sanctity in others, avoids it as much as possible. The palate of their soul is so spoiled that they are incurable. All their perfection is in their books, not in their souls where it ought to be their honor and glory. But what do we really find there? Nothing but selfishness. And yet we dare not declare our sincere feelings to them, for we would be met with mockery and derision. However, in these matters, those who are really spiritual must have the prudence of the serpent together with the simplicity of the dove. They should proceed with caution and not as fools, remaining attached to God and his divine will.

The experience of the wise should serve as a precaution to prevent us from falling into the misfortunes of those who have deserted religious solitude. Whoever avoids it is not a religious either in soul or in body. We know that flesh and blood, that creatures and little pleasures have carried even the best religious away from their essential spirit into what is accidental. They go to such excess that it becomes their final end. Like the blind on the edge of a precipice, they reach the point where they don't even know their obligations to strive for perfection and that they are to be more perfect than seculars. This is an infallible sign of great withdrawal from the spiritual means that lead to their salvation.

Now it would be a waste of time to try to convince such persons about the pleasure and advantages the soul receives from divine consolations when in solitude. The crude, animal man abhors this thought like a scourge, even to the point where he doesn't want to look into his conscience. He is afraid of the moral ruin he will find there, and consequently be obliged to return to God. As long as we don't talk to him about interior perfection and his soul, and as long as everything corresponds to his desires all will go well. When I see this I am strongly provoked to cry out to God at the top of my voice. Alas! This kind of person, exercises no discipline over his senses and is not concerned about what he says or does, as long as those whom he charms by his babbling consider him a good soul. Thus he lives in vanity, conceit and pretence. He is a flatterer who is guided only by carnal prudence which makes him abominable before God. Entire days are spent with seculars in either eating and drinking, or in talking about worldly things to the scandal of the good and of little ones.

It is a wonder that any religious at all preserves a love for the true spirit of religious life in the midst of all these adversaries, and remains resolved to be really spiritual in spite of them and even of hell itself. Although their number is small, it does not matter. These few sparks will help to keep the religious state alive to God's honor and glory. If they are calumniated and looked upon as useless folk, they should humble themselves, and accept these trials from the hand of God without reflecting upon the sad state

of their brethren. But this is where many fail in virtue. They complain inordinately, or even fail completely in their good resolve
for want of weighing well this truth, viz. that all who wish to live
devoutly in Jesus Christ must be strongly determined to suffer
every kind of persecution. Hence, it is quite evident that they
only want to live on the abundance of his table and not on the
bitterness of his chalice or of his cross. They would like to gain
heaven without paying anything for it. Although they promise God
marvelous things in their prayers, they are weak in suffering, and
fail time after time, giving in to their passions in contempt of God
and their own souls.

I will not dwell here on the cowardice of those who thus wish
to reconcile two masters, God and Belial, the spirit and the flesh.
Suffice it to say that, since these two masters are so different by
nature and condition, the true Lord who is God, does not want
such souls. Thus their sensual nature willingly takes them as its
slaves. And all this misfortune comes only for want of a desire
for God. He who observes the exercises of religious life sincerely
and faithfully is not too concerned as to whether he is loved or
hated by others. He lets all go their way, while he remains occupied
with God alone and does his duty.

There is no use speaking of renunciation to the man who has
only a good nature and lives in the senses. He will never know anything better than good works, and will never renounce himself as
he ought unless he sees that he is weak and has no means of performing such works. For this reason the active life, which lies
more in the senses than in reason, is very delightful to these people,
and they willingly endure many afflictions because they expect
great merit from it. But even here they are full of their own ways,
desires, plans and attachments, while remaining completely ignorant
of themselves and of real goodness. They never want to lose themselves even to a small extent, and if, at times, they do, through
persuasion, it is only with an extreme fear of losing their feelings
and their savour of God. Hence, they only abandon themselves
little by little, and as little as possible, because they cannot believe
that a life of renunciation, detachment and resignation is actually
a holy life.

(Souls called to solitude should not be urged unnecessarily into active work) When a religious is drawn to solitude by his religious exercises, it is good to leave him in his repose. There he will enjoy peace and endure many struggles. He should not be drawn into the broad and common way of men. Because, in conforming himself to them, he will be forced to some extent to leave his own limits. Although he may not seem to lose anything in these sorties, nevertheless, his affection will imperceptibly persuade him to enter into the ways of others. Thus his spirit will take more pleasure and delight in them than will be apparent. Now this is due to the fact that he is free to act and to speak, and believes it doesn't matter if he follows the ways of others, providing he remains within the limits of his own ways. Actually he does all things quite confidently during this time, but when he returns to solitude, he sees how his affection is drawn to the outside, to all those spiritual occupations.

Now even though these occupations are most praiseworthy, still solitude and silence will be constantly calling us into ourselves, and to a very naked and simple recollection of all our powers. There, through the images and forms which nature will arouse in us we shall see how important it is to dwell in solitude and silence, in the enjoyment of a simple repose, and completely absorbed in the contemplation of God.

When we are about to perform some activity we must do so with full liberty of spirit, and consider all the circumstances involved. At the same time we should be careful that our spirit does not suffer any ill consequences because of it. However, there is no complete remedy for this. Nature is so constructed that it would be impossible for the senses not to receive renewed vigor from such activity. And the senses always fight against the spirit.

Now let us suppose that a true solitary is sometimes called to external work. At such a time he ought to have some good book dealing with very simple subjects, so that, after work and conversation, he may be able to read something worthwhile. Above all, when he returns to solitude, he must not forget to do this reading, so that he may be immune to the influence of natural forms and images. When they have all been banished, he will again enter into a serene and simple repose. But let him avoid entering too much into the affairs of others, because the moment he does so, he will find himself withdrawn from his own path. Still, in spite of all this, he must not refuse to undertake active work when obedience, charity or necessity demand it.

(*Love of solitude*)   Each one must resolve to become as interior as possible, and to use every spiritual means for this purpose. But let him be careful not to become attached to any particular spiritual exercise, for God may draw him to some other practice. And, although he ought to have a great love for solitude, let him avoid becoming attached to it, because he must follow God and not himself. He must leave God for God's sake, especially when he knows what God wants of him. But outside of that, let him lead a solitary life as much as possible, and it will become sweet and savoury to him and give great pleasure to God. It is a source of great pleasure to a superior to have such solitaries, souls of perfect prayer and contemplation. They cherish and sanctify their external solitude by the practice of a holy life and by a continual occupation with God.

(*When is the soul perfectly prepared for external work?*)   When the Spirit of God rules within, it withdraws the soul far from all multiplicity. For by nature it is single and simple. Only when the soul is completely consummated in God by his divine touches is it ready for external things, and not sooner. Then, as they say, it is capable of going through heaven and earth. Therefore, they are greatly deceived who say it is a certain sign that one is very interior when he is careful to perform his external actions well, and that he can then be employed in everything as long as he feels a slight attraction for God.

(*Contemplation not opposed to action*)   Although contemplation is incomparably better than action, it is still very praiseworthy and most meritorious for you to have great compassion for the poor. Let your ardent charity be poured out to the full extent of your means, especially upon the sick and those who are too weak to beg. (*He is speaking to the Bishop of Revol*). Contemplation is not opposed to external action when it is a matter of assisting one's neighbor.

Here is an important piece of wisdom, viz. we must model our exterior according to the interior, for it is the right of the interior. gradually to draw the exterior to itself, and never the opposite. According to right and reason that which is most noble should attract what is less noble in order to exalt it in and by itself. Now all works of the external senses, in comparison with those of the interior, are only lead, while the latter are like pure gold. For, if they are performed with a rather high degree of acquired love, in the sight of God they are like fine diamonds and precious rubies. See then, where your treasure, your life, your action, your love, both interior as well as exterior, ought to be. Look for it there where it must be, and do not deliberately fail in this, unless you want to be the most ungrateful creature that was ever born. For you were born to become love by actually loving your Spouse.

(*The perfect life*) The perfect life is first of all active rather than contemplative. Then it is contemplative and active. For the spiritual means used by the soul are, for a long time, founded only upon human effort aided by the grace of God. Then little by little the soul advances in the knowledge of God and itself. But it remains in this state for a long time without making much progress. Such practices are only the beginning and very remote means in acquiring the spiritual life. For this life is not acquired by the soul's weak efforts alone, nor while it still lives only in itself. But when it has been touched by God in its lower powers, the experience of his fragrance and sweetness gives it a certain delightful and frequent desire to be united to him. Thus it resolves to love him ardently above all things no matter what the cost.

Before the desire for perfection can become strong and constant the soul must spend a long time knocking at the door by means of deep sighs, humiliations and prayers. After that, the good God, who has given it the grace and the desire to importune him thus, will open the door and receive it into his embraces according to its capacity and disposition. And in proportion as the soul feels itself drawn and touched, to that extent does it advance in a sincere and firm desire for God. Now it looks for occasions to exercise its loving desire. And the more persons it finds who are poor and miserable, the more honored it feels in being able to serve them.

I know quite well that the active life, as it is commonly understood, is looked upon only as a devout and corporal work of mercy performed for one's neighbor. But when it is accompanied by prayer, or better still, when it is the effect and fruit of prayer, such an active life is far more noble than one that stands alone. Indeed there is no comparison between the two. The former, because of its excellence, is said to be *"spiritually active."* The one does great things for God and for itself. The other, of which we are here speaking, often does apparently less, but in fact accomplishes a great deal more, because it looks to God and is inspired by his love alone. And yet, to be truthful, it is not any the less active or ardent in performing every possible good for the needs of its neighbor. With generosity and kindness, it embraces everyone who seeks its help. Its only pleasure is to please God by such works. This applies to kindred souls who live in the world. They too are very pleasing to God, and make great strides in the interior life according to the measure of their spiritual and corporal works. There you have the active life.

I would very much like to know what life many, who are consecrated to God, are actually living, whether it is contemplative or active. In my opinion, I think they are living neither the one nor the other. I am not speaking here of those who are completely distracted and live like animals; they are not only wanting in religious discipline, but even in physical discipline. Here I am speaking of well-behaved religious, who are exact in the practice of regular observance. Even though they practice mortification and prayer, and have received splendid gifts of God for a long time, many of them are actually far from practicing the kind of active life which lies in charity towards one's brethren. Of what use is it to pray twice a day or even more, and to live continually in God's presence if we do not lovingly assist our brother when he needs our help?

What do we see today in so many? How much sensuality and

fastidiousness: in health, sickness, clothing, sleeping, eating, keeping warm and other like practices? How many are never content with what is given them, and very often can hardly conceal it. They always want what is beautiful, what is good or the best, and a great deal of it, and anything that is good for their well-being. In all this there can be no question of poverty of spirit. Such persons consider themselves physicians, and want everyone to live after their fashion. But when it comes to giving assistance to the sick, they are like dead statues. And even if it is their duty by office, which they ought to perform cheerfully, they can hardly find the energy to provide for the urgent needs of their brothers. I do not mean that all should be equally suited for every task, but out of charity and compassion they should make a virtue of necessity and arouse a sincere enthusiasm for their tasks. But it is a pity to see how many are fastidious and wanting in compassion for the illnesses of their brothers. When it is a question of treating their wounds, ulcers and other common infections they lose heart. This is indeed far from having a cordial desire for such work. But then it is not surprising that those who have no virtue for themselves have none for others.

Good religious help their brothers even when obedience does not command. Now it is quite true that they should not hanker after many activities when they earnestly give themselves to occupation with God. Still, when they see immediate occasions, or when necessity absolutely demands it, they ought to assist their neighbor in his needs and for the moment set aside solitude and spiritual repose. But if they are often occupied in such work, they should notify their superiors, without their neighbor knowing it. Charity always knows how to set aside self and its own interests. For its sake, the soul is willing to lose its honor and to accept shame, confusion, complaints and insults. At this point, even the best fail. Because they are too attached to their honor, they refuse to help their brother when he is in urgent need. They are not sufficiently convinced of the great importance of their brother's pains and troubles. Here they might use a little prudence, and humbly inquire if he is in need or not. But the best thing to do is always to judge that he is in some need, measuring others by themselves. Not to do one's duty on such occasions, even though frequent, is to be far removed from that charity which lovingly desires and anticipates such occasions, or at least cordially looks forward to them.

1. John of St. Samson is speaking to religious, but the general principles apply to all Christians since they too are called to holiness and perfection.

2. Here the writer is speaking particularly of Carmelite communities.

CHAPTER VI

CONTEMPLATIONS ON THE BLESSED VIRGIN MARY[1]

Privileges and Prerogatives of Our Lady

O my Beloved, we must now consider one of the greatest wonders you created in heaven and earth, greater than all creatures. It is your beloved and blessed Mother, Mother of you, the God-Man. Where other creatures receive grace only in a limited degree, she received it in all its fullness. Men and angels receive it in widely varying degrees. The angels receive more than men. However, some men, your friends, receive more than the angels, and in a higher degree. But your blessed Mother possesses grace with the fullness of a sea, flowing into her from you its actual source, her Head, her Lord and Savior. Now, your grace reaches perfect fullness, which is all that God could ever bestow of himself. And from your fullness we have all received grace according to the measure and capacity of our love, and according to our disposition. But your blessed Mother received everything. Through the splendor of your grace she has become most illustrious and perfect. And now, for all eternity, she reigns at your right hand as your Mother, and as Queen and Mistress of all the universe. Through her enormous treasures she is filled with every splendor and beauty, both in body and in soul. Thus, according to the revelations of the Holy Spirit in the Scriptures, she is a wonder and a prodigy to the angels and saints in glory, as well as to your elect upon earth.

Therefore, without descending into more detailed considerations, I can say that she is all things in all creatures. She possesses all beauty, all gifts and all goodness even to the point of lavishing it upon others. Thus, as a pure creature ennobled to the highest degree and made illustrious by the sea of graces which you bestowed upon her, she is all and has all. In this capacity she rules eternally and in full splendor over all creatures as their Lady and Queen.

Just as she eminently surpasses every spirit because of her consummated grace, so also does she surpass all creatures in love, because she loves you with a boundless love. In her, grace can do nothing more, since she cannot receive any more graces. Her capacity is greater than that of all other creatures put together, and therefore, contains all graces. Nor can you bestow any more upon her, for she possesses all that you can give her.

O marvelous and most wonderful creature of this earth! You were created and made illustrious in the highest degree in order to reign as Spouse and Mother of the infinite God, and Queen over all creatures, even the angels, perfect as they are in their various hierarchies. O my Love, your marvels and prodigies enrapture us with infinite wonder. Thus in her and by her you receive more eternal delight than in all other creatures, because you made her your Mother. All creatures, both in heaven and on earth, honor her with the greatest reverence and humility, and serve her with great love and pleasure.

No one here below better portrays your infinite Person in all its majesty both interiorly and exteriorly in your words, actions and habits, than she does. By the living example of her life she becomes for us, as it were, another you. Hence, when we penetrate her perfections we penetrate your own. We see your goodness in hers, and your love in hers, just as we see her love and goodness in that of your own. Therefore, we should contemplate her as we do you, in her essential beauty and in the external manifestation of it. We should contemplate it above the purest, simplest, and most enriching speculation. For, if what is visible in her is beyond all understanding, that which is hidden in her is far more incomprehensible and cannot be understood in this life. Therefore, enraptured by this sight, we should admire, and contemplate it in the sweet calm of profound silence.

Moreover, she is the almoner of your vast and infinite treasures. She is the Mistress over them, because she is your most worthy Mother and the Queen of all creatures. Hence, she distributes them to all men and for all time. By her continual intercession you also distribute them at times according to our needs, and at other times out of pure kindness and love. All this is done in order to ennoble our poor nature with all the perfections and gifts necessary to sanctify us perfectly in this life and to attain the sublime state of glory in the next.

Let us not express our thoughts in any more detail, my Beloved, or descend to the particulars of her excellence. Let us remain enraptured by her essential beauty, which shines forth in all her words and actions, and by that beauty which is not visible externally, but always remains within her own essence. By this I mean her perfection, which she possesses in its highest plenitude. It was with this kind of perfection that she loved you in this life. For this reason she enjoys you more perfectly than all men put together. For in your glory, she, by herself, forms a very separate choir, distinct from all creatures.

But why do we portray her in so much detail, although it be so poorly and inadequately? Ah, my Life, it is for the purpose of giving you greater honor and glory in your Mother. We do this for your sake, because we know you are infinitely pleased to see your most humble servants and friends delighted and enraptured over the prodigies they contemplate in your Mother. That is why they are very often completely poured out in proclaiming to you her perfections and privileges, and her supreme magnificence as sovereign Mistress of all creatures, whether in heaven, on earth, or in hell. All revere her name. Good souls and the demons bend their knees and bow with respect. In all your vast eternity, my Beloved, after your name, nothing is sweeter than her name, her praises and privileges, her joy and her ineffable glory.

What more can we say of a being who is so perfect and accomplished in nature and grace that she is beyond all nature and grace? And what can we say of a soul who always enjoyed this perfection in a supereminent degree even while in the flesh? Certainly, my Love, we ought to be constantly transported over this subject and take infinite delight in thinking and speaking of her, as we admire the complete manifestation of yourself in her. Yes, we ought to be continually enraptured with her in order to speak of her rather than of any other creature, or even of all of them put together. From this most exalted glimpse of her we can easily see how she is like you more than all other creatures. For, to think and speak of her seems to be the same as thinking and speaking of you. Ah! How ineffable are the pleasure, glory and praise you receive through her! Who can ever describe them or define their limits? For there is no difference between you and her, except that she, of herself, is a creature, but super-excellent. However, the limits of her glory and magnificence do not by any means approach your own. I would like to explain this by some suitable comparison. But since there is no comparison, we shall do far better by comparing her grandeurs and perfections to the great arm of a sea. When it leaves the sea, it carries away everything with you as the most exalted and first idea among all your creatures, its unique and proper center. It is this flood of grandeurs and perfections of your holy Mother that transports us into its essence and will not permit us to leave it. There we see the essential habits of all her perfections, habits which produced continual acts throughout her earthly life. And they still continue their activity even in the state of eminent glory where she reigns forever in all of your eternity. This, my Love, is what we think of your Mother!

Behold our view of the super-excellent majesty of your Mother. To our amazement and exceeding admiration, she incomparably surpasses all things. Because of her profound and complete identity with you as the most exalted and first idea among all your creatures, it is impossible for any human sense or intelligence to grasp it. Hence, she has always been present to you such as she is in her actual existence. But, in order to complete and perfect this admirable design in her, you used all the means ordained for such an end according to your eternal fore-knowledge. You did it so effectively that she has never failed for a single moment to love you most ardently and to praise and contemplate you in an admirable manner. This was possible, because, on your part, my Love, you provided graces which always had their full effect, and she corresponded to them so well that she never lost touch with the infinite.

Therefore, your Mother, who is also our Queen and Mother,

always loved you with an equal and unchanging love. Such was
the effect of the grace with which she was adorned from the first
moment of her blessed conception. That is why she is your unique
Spouse, your all beautiful and spotless one. Alas, my Beloved, how
far are we other poor creatures from such grace and love! But
then love does not claim the same gifts and favors for us that
it claims for the Spouse and Queen of the eternal King, the Son
of God. Hence, after you, we take more delight in her than in
all the rest of the universe. For her we desire the greatest glory,
and hold in the greatest reverence all the favors, joys and honors
she enjoys in you.

If it were possible for us to give her what is naturally impossible,
namely, the same favors, the glory, joy and all that you yourself
possess, we would give it to her with the most ardent love. But
since we cannot do so, we at least declare that this sovereign
prodigy of love is worthy of perfect love from all creatures. You
have set her before us as someone who is to be constantly admired,
studied and contemplated as the most exalted expression of this
love in our creation and regeneration. For this singular favor,
we owe you the highest praise and thanksgiving. In heaven, the
blessed already enjoy the vision of their Mistress, while we who
are yet on earth must wait for this happiness. Although you will be
our essential happiness, she too will bring us happiness, an accidental happiness.

In conclusion, my Beloved, I wish to say that your Mother and
our Queen, was a greater mystic than any of your saints have ever
been or will be. Even in this life she saw and enjoyed your
immense riches and favors, for she was your most perfect follower.
The breadth and depth of her mystical life and of the many varied
expressions of it, as well as of her thoughts, are in a class by themselves, and far beyond any other mysticism. Being thus plunged
into the whole of your Being, for her, all things became a perfect
encounter with you. Hence, she performed all external actions with
a wisdom so divine that, in comparison with her, the greatest saints
were in their flight only like the birds of earth. Moreover, her
adornment was sovereignly perfect and in keeping with her state.
Then too, she had a full and infused knowledge suited to her

capacity, and as much as she needed in order to understand what she was obliged to know. Having become eminently perfect in your love and grace while in this life, she enjoys an even greater perfection in the state of your infinite glory. There she sees all things in you and in the most Holy Trinity in a more excellent and perfect manner than all the rest of the blessed put together.

(*Our Lady's Visit to St. Elizabeth*)   Blessed be Thou, my Love and my Life. For, while you were still enclosed in the virginal womb of your blessed Mother, you already fulfilled your duty as Savior to the greater glory of your eternal Father and the sanctification of men. For this reason your divine love inspired and excited your Mother to depart hastily to visit her cousin St. Elizabeth in order to lavish your holiness on the fruit of her womb, namely, St. John the Baptist. Now, it is quite true to say that the better one is by nature, the more he desires to give of himself. For it is the nature of goodness to communicate and lavish itself upon others as much as possible. And the more it gives itself, the more it desires to give. Here, let us speak of the loving effects of grace in your holy Mother, of those outpourings and communications that you delight in bestowing upon others through her.

Hence, I see you carried lovingly and joyfully by your Mother to purify the soul of your precursor, both through the abundance of your Spirit and through the holiness that pours out so delightfully from the mouth of your holy Mother. Her words, so full of love, light and abundant wisdom, are capable of transporting everyone she encounters, so that they become lost in her as in the profound depths of an infinite sea. They seem to feel that they become part of this sea in all its immensity.

It is for this reason that you hasten with your Mother to Zachary's house. There you dispose your chosen precursor, John the Baptist, to be filled with the fullness of your Spirit, of your grace, your love and your holiness. This was the first external work of your holy Humanity hidden in the womb of Mary. It is credible that this journey was not painful for her and, because of the great desire you gave her for it, was promptly carried out. Such had to be the effect of the overflowing love and joy with which you filled her. When the soul is intoxicated with love it is able to endure the most excrutiating torments and even death. Under the sweet violence of such a fire it considers the greatest pains and difficulties as nothing. Therefore, I am of the opinion that you did not permit her to suffer much on this journey and that she seemed almost to fly, so buoyant and quick was she.

Nevertheless, my Love, we cannot doubt that, in this journey, your Mother accomplished an admirable work, even though she was in a state of ecstasy, transported by you and your Spirit, and was no longer living in her cherished retreat at Nazareth. Although she loved solitude dearly, and in it would have enjoyed in greater peace the sacred treasure with which she was filled, in this encounter, she was not concerned over loss or gain. The fact is, she experienced great happiness in having you enclosed within her womb, and in being continually overwhelmed with love and joy.

Actually, during this journey, she enjoyed great recollection and interior simplicity. As for her exterior, she paid attention only to what was necessary to find her way. For this holy Virgin, being the Mother of such a Son, should be a divine spirit, even in her external bodily actions, rather than a pure and natural creature, like those who have only the gifts and the habits of a well ordered nature for their perfection. Such is my opinion, my Beloved, and I cannot give your Mother a lesser excellence. Since she actually and personally carried you, you inspired and filled her beyond measure with your Spirit and with all his gifts. This is not surprising since it was entirely in keeping with the order and nature of the most Holy Spirit and of your superabundant grace.

Indeed, since this grace elevates many other lesser creatures to an exalted and intimate union with him, it is only right to believe that its effects were far greater in your blessed Mother. In a most extraordinary manner, you yourself produce these effects in her, effects that are most worthy of you and most conformed to your infinite majesty. You could not do less than overwhelm her with every kind of blessing, and grace in the superabundance of your Spirit and love. Therefore, who can be astonished at the cheerful agility of your Mother, since it is an effect of such a cause? The Holy Spirit expresses it quite aptly under this similitude:

"See how the virgin comes over the mountains, skipping from mount to mount, like a little fawn and a gazelle" (*See how he comes leaping over the mountains and beyond the hills like the fawns and the gazelles*" Song of Songs 2, 8-9) Could he have better expressed your love's great desire to produce its effects than by this charming comparison?

But, my Love, we must now plunge into new excesses and wonders over what takes place here as you manifest your infinite love through your Mother. We must see how this most pure Virgin, now virginally fruitful by the complete overshadowing of the Holy Spirit, bears you within her with infinite honor and reverence. She is completely transported and lost in the abyss of your divinity, and most profoundly absorbed in the wondrous prodigy accomplished in her. We must also contemplate her as she begins to perform her duty in and by you, seeing how she greets her cousin with a loving kiss, speaking words of life and love, words of indefinable pleasure to her. For her part, St. Elizabeth is overwhelmed by the Holy Spirit with a sweet and delightful intoxication. As he pours himself out upon the child enclosed in her womb, the infant leaps with joy and inexpressible exultation, thus giving expression to what he already felt and saw by experience.

These, my Beloved, are all miracles. Again, it is another prodigy to see how the supernatural powers of St. Elizabeth and of St. John sustain the sweet influence of your Spirit and your ravishing love. For they were filled with great abundance. Ravished with profound wonder and under the overwhelming influence of the divine Spirit, St. Elizabeth says to your Mother, "From whence comes this honor to me that the Mother of my Lord comes to me?" Suffice it to say that this is the expression of a very full and pure jubilation. It is a great wonder how these blessed souls were able to sustain it without dying, so strong was the touch of grace upon them. In this scene there is infinitely more to contemplate than to speculate.

Although we may be able to reflect on their external effects to some extent, we must contemplate these hidden abysses with profound wonder and silence. In this mystery we see what St. John wanted to say through the exultation which he manifested in the womb of his mother. He would have liked very much to pass beyond the maternal enclosure, if it were permitted him, in order to adore you before all the world as his God, his Lord and Savior. He was astonished over the favor he then received from you. Therefore, my Love, behold your servant, John the Baptist. His reason and knowledge were so fully developed and he was so filled with your divine Spirit that, were he born then, and had he attained a competent age and strength, he would have been as ready as ever to go and preach you, and to proclaim penance to all men.

All aspects of this mystery are ineffable in their savor. We are struck with profound admiration over all the mysterious circumstances contained in it. They move on quite simply from one to another, from splendor to splendor, from one abyss to another, constantly producing new excesses and wonders in simple souls. See what the marvels of God and the outpourings of his grace and love can accomplish in his cherished friends. See too what these friends in turn accomplish in him and in his love with the riches bestowed upon them. Behold the effect of God's love on his creature and the return of that love, flowing back to you, my Beloved, its infinite sea. But this work is done more in secret than in public, because it is more expedient, being so ordained by your eternal foreknowledge.

What took place here between these two mothers is beyond words. Only silence, looking and tasting can discover something of it for us. For it is a fire. Its strong and diffusive action causes another fire. Then both of them are united and blended, so to speak, in your fire, so that they no longer exist except in you. O holy and worthy Mothers, who merited to receive such an ineffable favor!

Now, my Lord, let us hear your blessed Mother's reply to her dear cousin. "My soul," she says, "magnifies the Lord and my spirit rejoices in God my salvation." And she continues this canticle which contains the great mysteries of love that you accomplished in her. She attributes them to you with a profound humility and with an equally profound and simple love. If, after this, your humble and loving orator wants to probe and penetrate them, he will find abundant delights concealed under exalted thoughts.

Moreover, it is surprising that you and your Mother stayed on in this home. This was done to practice contemplation and for the mutual love of the two mothers. Being greatly inflamed, their love became a source of great delight and an ineffable savor. For they spent the best part of the day and perhaps the night in a transport of love over the incomparable favors they had received from you, and were melted in the immense sea of your love.

How happy would we have been to see and hear these two mothers, so fruitful and so rich, engaged in a conversation that was more divine than human! I say they were rich, because their souls were so filled with love and holiness that they sent each other into ecstasy. But your blessed Mother especially ravished the soul and the attention of her dear cousin with the sweet impetuosity of her love. Unable to admire sufficiently the charming sweetness and flow of her love, she was in a state of constant wonder over this prodigious mystery. For it contains in itself the abysses of other infinite mysteries, mysteries that were to play an important part in the redemption of the human race, especially in the exalted sanctification of your Majesty's most favored elect. These insights were the subjects of discussion as well as the delight of these holy mothers, neither being sufficiently able to admire your prodigal love and goodness.

At this time too, it is only right that your blessed Mother should assist her dear cousin at the birth of her son. This she does with all joy, respect and reverence, considering it a pleasure to render her this kind of service.

---

1. This chapter is translated from the French text as it appears in **Devotio Mariana,** by Valerius Hoppenbrouwers, O.Carm., Carmelite Institute, (Rome, 1960); cf. pp. 354-383.

GLOSSARY

Abstraction—withdrawal or detachment of the soul from the senses, and a recollection of its faculties within itself, centering them upon God. (cf. chap. on *Aspiration, p. 102).

Anagogical—comes from the Greek, *ana* (up), and *ago* (to lead). Among spiritual writers of the 15th and 16 centuries, aspirations were also called anagogical movements, because they raise the soul up to God by means of a loving impulse or flight. John of St. Samson applies the term usually to the more advanced type of aspiration, viz., aspirations which are spiritual, rapid, very short and ardent. This form of aspiration or anagogical act implies ease and a quick flight of the soul. Such acts, he says, quickly raise the soul to delightful union with God and lead to loving ecstasies. (cf. chap. on *Aspiration, p. 86)

Animal man—refers to life lived on the level of the senses.

Dilate, to—to enlarge, open wide, expand; to give the soul greater freedom and ease in performing interior acts, e.g. acts of love, faith, abandonment, etc. *"To dilate the soul,"* means to fill the soul with an expansive love that overflows with affection for its Beloved.

Essential aspiration—appears to be an advanced form of aspiration reduced to its essential elements, viz., very brief, ardent, quick and frequent, but capable of lifting the soul up entirely into God cf. chap. on *Aspiration, p. 97). It is for souls who are in the stage of simplified prayer (cf. *ibidem, p. 17). Elsewhere John of St. Samson describes it as a simple, burning glance and a brief, wordless longing (cf. *ibi. p. 100) ; or, as a simple inclination and heartfelt desire that is very spiritual (p. 107) ; a great and ardent love that enables the soul to form very simple and wonderful elevations (p. 102).

Exemplarism—a doctrine which teaches that all created beings existed eternally in the divine essence as in their exemplar.

They were always present in God's thought as in the arche-type and model according to which they were created. Being conformed to the divine idea, all created beings, before their creation, were one with the essence of God, just as ideas are one with the intelligence that conceives them. (cf. Pourrat, *"La Spiritualité Chrétienne,"* Vol. II, p. 363). John of St. Samson, following Ruysbroeck, maintained that there is a close relationship between the creature and its original image, for the creature is made according to it. Now since created life comes from God, it also aspires to be reunited to God again, to flow back into the original image. This need to find oneself again, united to the original image is the foundation of the spiritual life and of the theory of introversion (cf. Janssen, O. Carm., *"Les Origines de la Reforme des Carme en France au 17th Siecle,"* pp. 236-239). Once the soul has re-entered itself even to its depths, thanks to the transformation, it is united to its first Image, which is its original ground (*depth*), and is nothing else than God Himself. There, united to God, it participates in the very life of God. (cf. *"Oeuvres de Jean de St. Samson,"* I, p. 170, col. 2, B-E.).

Introversion—from the Latin *intro* (within), and *versus* (turned towards). In mystical theology it means that the mind is turned within to converse with God dwelling in the soul. Thus it means recollection.

Irradiation—illumination, enlightenment, ray of divine light (cf. chap. on *Aspiration*, p. 104).

Supereminent—in the writings of John of St. Samson it is equivalent to super-essential, but sometimes it is used to express an act performed with the highest perfection, e.g. "acts of super-eminent admiration for the Beloved."

Superessential—when this term is used in reference to God's own life, e.g. "the superessential bosom of the Spouse" (cf. *Aspiration*, p. 80) it means the deepest depths of the divine nature. When it is used in reference to the soul's spiritual life, e.g. "enjoyment of the superessential life," John of St. Samson means the highest state of perfection, viz., the transforming union. John here depends directly upon Ruysbroeck and Henry

Herp who use the term in reference to the psychological elements of mystical experience. To avoid the danger of misunderstanding, spiritual masters of the 17th century used the term "supereminent" as an equivalent, as does John of St. Samson.

Transfusion—soul is poured out into God. It is equivalent to transformation into God.

Wonder—i.e. admiration, astonishment, amazement. This state of mind belongs to a form of contemplation in which the activity of the understanding is so simplified that it *looks* at the beloved Object in wonder and admiration. It is a simple gaze upon the truth. Here we have the *loving attention* spoken of by St. John of the Cross when describing acquired contemplation. It also belongs to infused contemplation, when the soul *"stands* idle with an inclined spirit and with open eyes, but without reflection" (cf. Ruysbroeck, *Sparkling Stone*, trans. by Dom Wynschenk, p. 210). St. Teresa identifies it with the *prayer of quiet*. She speaks of admiration, as being the soul's reaction before the marvels shown it by God in certain imaginary and intellectual visions (cf. *Life*, c. 37) ; it is particularly evident in ecstasy (*ibi*. c. 20). John of St. Samson also considers *wonder* and *admiration* as a form of contemplation; e.g. "contemplate your infinite Object with great *wonder* by means of a simple gaze, and in profound silence" (cf. chap. on *Aspiration*, p. 100). Elsewhere, speaking of souls who enjoy such prayer, John says, "they keep the eye of their understanding open to look with *admiration* and pleasure upon him who draws them to himself" (*ibi*. p. 103 ; also chap. on *Contemplation*, p. 126).

BIBLIOGRAPHY

BOUCHEREAUX (DR. SUSANNE), *La Reforme des Carmes en France et Jean de Saint-Samson*, Paris, 1950, 490 pp. Contains a thorough bibliography.

BRANDSMA (TITUS), O. Carm., *Carmelite Mysticism*, Chicago, Carmelite 1936, 113 pp.

BREMOND (L'ABBE HENRI), *Histoire litteraire du sentiment religieux en France depuis la fin des guerres de religion jusqu'a nos jours*, Paris, 1919-1936, 11 vols. and 1 vol. index; cf. vol. II, pp.332-343; 379ff.

DONATIEN DE ST. NICOLAS, O. Carm., *La Vie, les maximes et partie des oeuvres du Fr. Jan de S. Samson*, Paris, Denis Thiery, 1651, 533 pp.

HEALY (MOST REV. KILIAN), O. Carm., *Methods of prayer in the Directory of the Carmelite Reform of Touraine*, Rome, 1956, 184 pp.

JANSSEN (P.W.), O. Carm., *Les Origines de la Reforme des Carmes en France au XVIIe Siecle* Martinus Nijhoff, Hague, 1963, 291 pp. Contains an excellent bibliography.

JEAN DE SAINT-SAMSON (Frère), O. Carm., *Les Oeuvres spirituelles et mystiques du divin contemplatif F. Jean de S. Samson ... avec un abrégé de sa vie*, recueilly et composé par le P. Donatien de S. Nicolas, O. Carm., Rennes, 1658-1659, 2 t.

—— *Directions pour la vie interieure*. Choix établi et présenté par Dr. Susanne Bouchereaux, Paris, Editions du Seuil, 1948, 271 pp.

—— *Light on Carmel*, An anthology from the Works of John of St. Samson, based on the French edition of Sernin de St. André, O.C.D., ... edited in Dutch by Albert Groeneveld, O. Carm., ... translated by Joachim Smet, O. Carm. ... in *The Sword*, Carmelite quarterly, vol. 5, n. 4, Oct. 1941.

JOSEPH OF JESUS, O. Carm., *Grandes Carmes de Rennes. Vie de F. Jean de Saint-Samson, Carme.*, Grand couvent de Rennes,

XVIIᵉ siecle, Manuscript, pp. 195. Strictly speaking it is not a Life of John of Saint-Samson, but a collection of documents, letters, testimonies and personal remembrances.

SERNIN DE ST. ANDRE, O.C.D., *Vie du V. F. Jean de Saint-Samson,* Paris Poussielgue, 1881, 392 pp. This work uses the MS of Father Joseph and the Life written by Father Donatien, but adds nothing new to these works.

VILLIERS (C. DE), O. Carm., *Bibliotheca Carmelitana,* new edition by G. Wessels, O. Carm., 2 t. in 1 vol., Rome, 1927.

An Interesting Thought

The publication you have just finished reading is part of the apostolic efforts of the Society of St. Paul of the American Province. A small, unique group of priests and brothers, the members of the Society of St. Paul propose to bring the message of Christ to men through the communications media while living the religious life.

If you know of a young man who might be interested in learning more about our life and mission, ask him to contact the Vocation Office in care of ALBA HOUSE, at 2187 Victory Blvd., Staten Island, New York 10314. Full information will be sent without cost or obligation. You may be instrumental in helping a young man to find his vocation in life. *An interesting thought.*